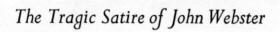

The Tragic Satire of John Webster

THE TRAGIC
SATIRE OF
W~JOHN
EBSTER

by Travis Bogard

Glories, like glow-wormes,
afarre off shine bright
But lookt to neare,
have neither heat nor light.

NEW YORK
RUSSELL & RUSSELL · INC
1965

BRESCIA COLLEGE
LIBRARY
30086

COPYRIGHT, 1955, BY
THE REGENTS OF THE UNIVERSITY OF CALIFORNIA
REISSUED, 1965, BY RUSSELL & RUSSELL, INC.
BY ARRANGEMENT WITH THE UNIVERSITY OF CALIFORNIA PRESS
L. C. CATALOG CARD NO: 65-13952

PRINTED IN THE UNITED STATES OF AMERICA

To
My Father and Mother

PREFACE

THE TRAGIC VISION OF JOHN WEBSTER — *that knowledge of human suffering which found its expressive form in his twin tragedies,* The White Devil *and* The Duchess of Malfi — *is the general subject of this book. It has been treated briefly in many essays by various critical hands, and at greater length in the commentary to F. L. Lucas' edition of Webster's complete works and in the book-length studies of E. E. Stoll* (John Webster: The Periods of His Works as Determined by His Relations to the Drama of His Day), *Rupert Brooke* (John Webster and the Elizabethan Drama), *and Clifford Leech* (John Webster).

It would be possible at this juncture to echo the words of Flamineo in The White Devil *and say,*

> *I do not look*
> *Who went before, nor who shall follow me;*
> *No, at my self I will begin and end.*

Yet the readers of other critics of Webster will see the many ways in which my study has built on theirs, and I can do no better than borrow another phrase from Webster, and ask that what I have written may be read "by their light." I should add that it is chiefly by the light of Professor Lucas' commentaries that I have read Webster himself.

I have attempted to approach Websterian tragedy in two ways:

first, historically, in an effort to read his work accurately in accordance with the conventions of Jacobean tragedy, and to clear away certain preconceptions about the dramatist who is traditionally held to be "second to Shakespeare"; and second, critically, without detailed reference to any period, setting forth re-creatively yet systematically the scope and significance of Webster's tragic vision.

His particular greatness as a dramatist does not, I feel, result from the incontestible (and often-cited) eloquence of his verse. Comment on his language has no very great place in the present study for the simple reason that the verse speaks for itself. Even William Archer, Webster's most resolute enemy, knew this and said so. It is great verse and needs no justifying commentary. What Archer would not admit is that Webster had any claim to the title of dramatist or that he had a consistent philosophic vision of the world of his experience. A satisfactory answer must, I believe, view the two counts of Archer's indictment as a single issue, because the dramaturgy of a tragic writer must be essentially determined not by play-making formulas but by that shaping vision of experience without which no play can be more than melodrama.

There is little in Professor Stoll's study of Webster's affiliation with the drama of his time or in Rupert Brooke's description of the general characteristics of Webster's verse style which can be advanced as an argument against the position Archer represents. Professor Lucas answers Archer with the historical explanation that Webster's dramaturgy was adequate to his time. Yet this is substantially what Archer admitted when he began his attack on the Jacobean drama—an attack for which, apparently, Webster was the sacrosanct Shakespeare's whipping boy. Neither Professor Lucas' explanation, nor Dr. Leech's evidence that the tragedies contain excellent acting roles is, to my mind, quite adequate to establish the essential point: that tragic dramaturgy

*and tragic vision are interdependent. The opinion here offered
is that Webster was a great dramatist because, seeing the world
with both pity and contempt, he remained faithful to his vision
by blending two almost incompatible genres, tragedy and satire.*

*By itself his tragedy is limited, personal, descending even to
melodrama. His satire is frequently conventional and unimpres-
sive. Yet neither satire nor tragedy alone could fully express
his complex response to the world. The points of view and the
expressive methods of both satire and tragedy were necessary
for him to set forth truly his tragic conception of human life. It
is the vitality of the heroic story which lends force and relevance
to the satire's mockery; and, in turn, it is the satire which provides the heroic story with the generality necessary to all great
tragedy. Webster's chief power as a dramatist lies in his skillful
control of the difficult integration of genres which tragic satire
demands.*

*The notes contain full bibliographical citations of the books
from which I have quoted. For the sake of uniformity I have
modernized all spellings, except where such normalization would
alter the metrical arrangement of the line (e.g., "Oh the rare
tricks of a Machivillian!"). The capitalization and punctuation
of the editors remain unchanged except in a few minor instances:
the third person singular verb form ("return's") has been spelled
without the apostrophe. Unless an emendation seems highly
conjectural, I have silently omitted the square brackets of the
various editors.*

*To list the numerous articles and reviews of performances, to
name the tangentially related studies—the dramatic essays of
T. S. Eliot, for instance, or Harley Granville-Barker's* Prefaces
to Shakespeare*—which have at one time or another crossed the
path of this work and changed its shape or direction, would be
to increase the pagination by more than economy dictates. These
works are generally known to all students of drama, or, if they*

are not, can easily be discovered in the standard bibliographies.

I wish to thank the following publishers for permission to quote excerpts from various publications: Columbia University Press, Elizabethan and Jacobean Playwrights, *by H. W. Wells, New York, 1939;* Henry E. Huntington Library, Comicall Satyre and Shakespeare's Troilus and Cressida, *by O. J. Campbell, San Marino, California, 1938; The* Macmillan Company, Essays, *by W. B. Yeats, New York, 1924; The* New Yorker, *"Notes on London at the End of a War," by Edmund Wilson, June 2, 1945;* Oliver and Boyd, Ltd., Plays of John Marston, *edited by H. Harvey Wood, Edinburgh, 1934–1939;* Oxford University Press, The Complete Works of John Webster, *edited by F. L. Lucas, New York, 1937 (permission granted by the editor and the publisher);* Oxford University Press, Shakespeare's Satire, *by O. J. Campbell, New York, 1943;* Routledge and Kegan Paul, Ltd., The Plays and Poems of George Chapman, *edited by Thomas Marc Parrott, London, 1910.*

More personally, I acknowledge with gratitude the help I have received from Professor Gerald Eades Bentley of Princeton University, Professor Willard Farnham and Professor B. H. Lehman of the University of California at Berkeley, and Professor Imogen B. Walker of Mills College. Their counsel at different stages has materially aided in making the way smooth. I shall always feel a particular indebtedness to Professor Edward Hubler of Princeton University, under whose direction my studies of Webster were initiated and encouraged, and to Professor Brewster Rogerson of Kansas State College, who has been, in a sense I think he will understand, the Bosola of this undertaking.

TRAVIS BOGARD

Contents

INTRODUCTION   1

PART ONE: *The Tragic Design*

Chapter One: Webster and Chapman   13
    "Things like truth"   14
    "Most sententious Tragedy"   19
    The Tragedy of the Complete Man   21
    Chapman's Tragic Action   26

Chapter Two: Webster's Tragic Action   35
    "Integrity of life"   38
    The Individual in the Type   44
      The Soliloquy   44
      The Character   48
      Motivation   50

Chapter Three: The Tragic Characters   57
    Vittoria and Flamineo   57
    The Duchess and Bosola   63

PART TWO: *The Satiric Design*

Chapter Four: Webster and Marston   85
   The Revenge of Virtue on Vice   88
   Tragedy and Satire   96

Chapter Five: Satiric Counterpoint to the Tragic Action 99
   Sententia and Fable   102
   Choral Comment   105
   Contrasting Action   111
   Contrasting Tone   112

Chapter Six: The Satiric Panorama   117
   "The skull beneath the skin"   117
   "Courtly reward and punishment"   119
   "A perspective that shows us hell"   131
   Death and the Dignity of Man   141

Conclusion: Tragic Satire   147

NOTES AND REFERENCES   151

INTRODUCTION

THE LITERARY DEPENDENCE of John Webster on his contemporaries and immediate predecessors is both astonishing and annoying. At a time when every writer had in him something of the literary thief, when, indeed, verbal borrowing was routine and scarcely worth comment, Webster developed plagiarism to a fine art. He became the Raffles in a nest of upstart crows, surpassing all others in the virtuosity with which he culled fine phrases, moral maxims, and striking dramatic situations from Sidney, Montaigne, and his leading fellow workers in the drama and elsewhere. The fact has long been noted[1] and variously interpreted. It can be said of his practice, as F. L. Lucas suggests, that Webster generally betters what he borrows: at the very least, he weaves the words of other men so skillfully into his context that they become an integral part of his own fabric. Although the extent and frequency of his imitation seem unusual, the ability with which he shaped such borrowings to his own purposes, altering them to conform with his characteristic cadences and imagery, is equally unusual. The degree of transmutation is perhaps sufficient justification of his plagiaristic activities.

Such alchemy is remarkable; yet, to the critic seeking to understand Websterian tragedy, it is likely to be troublesome and

(1)

even misleading. The most immediately apparent of Webster's borrowings are those from Shakespeare, particularly the cluster associated with the madness of Cornelia in the fifth act of *The White Devil*. Webster's imitation here is so obvious that almost inevitably critic and general reader alike tend to think of Websterian tragedy in Shakespearian terms. Certainly, the resemblances conditioned Lamb's commentary on Webster in his *Specimens of English Dramatic Poets*. In this work, which served to rescue Webster, together with many of his contemporaries, from the oblique condemnation of oblivion, Lamb quoted extensively from the Cornelia scenes and in his notes stressed the comparison between the dramatists. After Lamb, the names of Webster and Shakespeare were inextricably linked, and, for more than a century thereafter, Webster was compared both to his advantage and disadvantage with the greater dramatist.

Clearly, there were factors other than Webster's imitation which led to this coupling. Webster's tragic protagonists were comparable in brilliance only to Shakespeare's. No one else had come so close to creating a second Cleopatra or Lady Macbeth as Webster had with Vittoria Corombona. The Duchess of Malfi had no peer in beauty and womanliness but in Shakespearian drama. It appeared further that Webster was comparable— some said equal—to Shakespeare in his power to create scenes of pathos, and the critics cited the deaths of Cornelia and Isabella, and of the Duchess and her children. Even if Webster's characterization and pathos were found by some to be far below Shakespeare's, his adherents could still make a claim for his language. His verse, to which the borrowings seemed "native and endowed," set him apart from and above his merely mortal contemporaries. On this point alone, comparison with Shakespeare was inevitable, and it is not surprising to find that to Lamb and to most of the critics who followed, Webster was more interesting, more justifiable, as a poet than as a playwright. It frequently appears that the brilliance of his verse rather than the dramatic strength of his tragedies has entitled him to a position in the pantheon of English tragic writers "second to Shakespeare."

Starting, therefore, with the borrowings from Shakespeare, and proceeding to a comparison of the two writers not as tragic dramatists but as tragic poets, Webster critics, at least in the nineteenth century, split into violently opposed factions. Webster's reputation became what might be called schizo-critical. At one extreme, Swinburne asserted that Webster was a true tragic artist, whose "station is at Shakespeare's right hand." At the other, Canon Charles Kingsley, weighing both Shakespeare and Webster in the balance of Victorian morality, found that Websterian tragedy lacked insight, and showed no trace "of that development of human souls for good or evil, which is Shakespeare's especial power." Such drama, he concluded, is the work "of the devil, and to the devil let it go." The choice was between Christ and Satan, and the consequences were probably inescapable. For, when critics more aware of the requirements of the theater turned their attention to Webster's dramaturgy, the comparison with Shakespeare was firmly in their minds. Placed beside his "master," Webster appeared as a "feeble and foolish" playwright. George Henry Lewes made the point clearly. He wrote of *The Duchess of Malfi* that it "is not the work of a dramatist; it is clumsy ignorance. [It] is a nightmare, not a tragedy. . . . If Shakespeare is a great dramatist, Webster and company are not dramatists at all; and nothing exalts him more than to measure him by his contemporaries."[2] Thus Archer, offering to substitute the dramaturgy of *The Green Goddess* for that of *The White Devil;* thus Shaw; thus numberless others.

The assumption was easy: Webster had imitated Shakespeare's language and therefore was imitating his dramatic methods. The

conclusion was inevitable: judged by the methods of Shakespearian tragedy, Webster was a maladroit hack. Perhaps naturally, no one noticed that the basic methods of Websterian tragedy are not imitative of Shakespeare's, that, in fact, Webster had
allied himself with playwrights who had aims and methods fundamentally different from their greatest contemporary—playwrights
who probably would not have imitated the design of Shakespearian tragedy even had they been capable of it.[3]

Many recent critics have noted that Websterian tragedy is
closely allied in one way or another to the tragedies of Chapman,
Marston, Jonson, and Tourneur.[4] They have stressed not only
that Webster borrowed phrases and situations from these dramatists, but also that he, like many of his contemporaries, was
writing tragedies which were in part satire and which revealed
an intense concern for specific evils of the world he knew. Henry
W. Wells, for instance, observes: "In writing another scourge of
villainy Webster is merely developing with new variations a
theme cultivated by the bitter Kyd, the morose Marston, the
savage Tourneur, the sardonic Middleton. Ben Jonson had dis-
closed the crimes of ancient Rome in serious plays much like
Webster's satirical tragedies of modern Italy. Webster, in short,
uncovers a nest of villains in the spirit of his predecessors and
in the severest tradition of Christian morality."[5] The truth of
this is, I think, generally admissible; yet if the question be asked,
Why is Webster a greater tragic writer than Kyd, Marston,
Tourneur, Middleton, or Jonson? the answer from many might
well be as it was in the nineteenth century: Because he was a
better poet than the others and because, satiric intention aside,
he modeled his tragedies after "his master Shakespeare" rather
than the others. Or, as Professor Wells continues his discussion
of Webster's relation to his predecessors: "His plays come nearer
to pure tragedy than theirs because of his ampler share of poetry,
nobility, and sympathy and because by virtue of this sympathy

they contain fine strokes of characterization, yet they miss the
perfection attained by his master Shakespeare largely because
they remain on the whole satirical essays and moral onslaughts
upon mankind rather than impartial tokens of human fate."[6]

The conception that Shakespeare was Webster's master appears to depend from the century of somewhat obfuscating criticism which followed Lamb's commentary. It is repeated so
frequently today as to require comment. Particularly it should be
noted that when, in *Troilus and Cressida* and *Timon of Athens,*
Shakespeare undertook to write what Professor Wells calls "satirical essays and moral onslaughts upon mankind," he was not
clearly his own master, let alone Webster's. Certainly, when
writing satire, he did not write tragedy. Webster did. Shakespeare could incorporate satire and misanthropic invective into
his tragedy, but he did not make it part of the general view of
the action. In Shakespearian tragedy the satiric voice is finally
silenced.

Webster, in two plays, made the satiric voice coequal with the
tragic, and in doing so brought together and steadily controlled
two all-but-incompatible attitudes toward human experience. It
is by virtue of this blending—really by virtue of the presence of
the satire—that Webster's plays can justifiably be called in any
degree tragedy. "Poetry, nobility, and sympathy" they have in
amplitude; but the poetry belongs equally to murderer and victim, the whores have nobility, and the sympathy of Webster for
Bosola as he murders the Duchess is no easily definable attitude.
By itself the tragic scheme is not much beyond morally confusing
melodrama. It is particular, local, temporary. Only when the
satiric counterpointing to the tragic plan is introduced does
Websterian tragedy achieve the generalized and universal level
of, in Professor Wells's term, "pure tragedy." Even then, it is
probably not "pure." Tragedy and satire together usher an
audience into a strange, morally ambiguous world. That the

audience does not turn from it in disgust is probably sufficient evidence of Webster's mastery, "second to none," of tragic satire.

Although he was not in any profound sense an imitator of Shakespeare, Webster was deeply influenced by the work of certain of his contemporaries, and, in order that his plays may be rightly understood, his allegiances to these contemporaries must be explored.

The preliminary note "To the Reader" is in the nature of a critical preface to *The White Devil*. The indictment against it on the grounds of its second-hand Latin, its derivative devotion to Senecan tragedy, its borrowed attitude of scorn for "the uncapable multitude," and its suggestion of the literary poseur may be valid. The opinions it formulates are apparently derived from those of Jonson set forth in the preface, "To the Readers," of *Sejanus*. Jonson observes that his play departs from the strict unity of time, and does not use the chorus, since the public no longer looks upon it with delight. Yet, he adds:

> If in truth of Argument, dignity of Persons, gravity and height of Elocution, fulness and frequency of Sentence, I have discharged the other offices of a *Tragic* writer, let not the absence of these *Forms* be imputed to me, wherein I shall give you occasion hereafter (and without my boast) to think I could better prescribe, than omit the due use, for want of a convenient knowledge.

Jonson seems to be pointing out his departures from classical formalities for two reasons: first, he fears, since his play is faithful in many but not all details, that his critics may cavil at the aberrations; and second, he intends later to adhere more strictly to classic precedent.

The relationship of Jonson's statements to his work is apparent, but the relevance of Webster's echoing these remarks is not so clear. To be sure, both dramatists were in a sense apologizing

for plays that failed in stage performance, and both were reori-
enting them for the benefit of the more "capable" reading public.
To justify a play, however, that bears so little resemblance to
classical tragedy as *The White Devil,* by pointing out that it has
no chorus or *nuntius,* and that it does not observe the critical
laws, seems totally irrelevant, and perhaps suggests a pose. Yet
it is not certain that Webster is defending his play or even suggesting that he should have written in the classical vein: "If it
be objected this is no true Dramatic Poem, I shall easily confess
it, . . . willingly, and not ignorantly, in this kind have I faulted."
And he continues to score the audience which not only objected
to his play, but which *also* would poison "the most sententious
Tragedy that ever was written." Lucas suggests, plausibly
enough, that the sententious tragedy which Webster had in mind
was *Catiline,* published in 1611, a year before the publication
of *The White Devil,*[7] and that Webster here is defending Jonson
as well as himself. Be this as it may, Webster is making no false
claims for himself or for his tragedy. Instead, he appears to be
aligning himself with Jonson in defense of the worth of the tragic
writer, and justifying the publication of plays which have in them
matters of more serious import than can readily meet the eye
and ear in the public theaters. In this he followed not only Jonson but Chapman and Marston, who, although sure of the worth
of their plays, felt it necessary to justify their publication.

Webster thus sides with dramatists who, whatever their individual differences, were concerned with establishing tragedy as a
fine art, were willing to take it seriously as of more than momen-
tary concern, and were seeking in their critical statements as well
as in their practice to justify publicly their belief in the dignity
of the tragic writer.

Corroboration of this view of Webster as a literary artist,
concerned for the worth of his tragedies, is supplied by the same
prefatory letter, in which he singles out for special attention the

two Jacobean writers who were most explicit about their dramatic intentions, and who had demonstrated themselves to be writing in accordance with well-conceived, fully formulated theories of drama.

> Detraction is the sworn friend to ignorance: For mine own part I have ever truly cherished my good opinion of other men's worthy Labours, especially of that full and heightened style of Master *Chapman:* The labour'd and understanding works of Master *Jonson:* The no less worthy composures of the both worthily excellent Master *Beaumont* & Master *Fletcher:* And lastly (without wrong last to be named) the right happy and copious industry of M. *Shakespeare,* M. *Dekker,* & M. *Heywood,* wishing what I write may be read by their light.

Webster makes no explicit evaluation of the work of Beaumont and Fletcher, Shakespeare, Dekker, or Heywood. That they work hard and write fluently and well is mere compliment. The praise of Jonson and Chapman, however, is of another order. If not evaluative, it is at least specific, and suggests that Webster felt a special allegiance to their work.

Of his relationship to Jonson, enough has been said to convey the full sense of the phrase "laboured and understanding." Webster did not quarry extensively from the texts of *Sejanus* and *Catiline.* A few verbal borrowings appear,[8] but Webster does not seem to have depended on Jonson for specific details or for suggestions pertinent to the design and conduct of the action. Rather, he admired the sentential accuracy and the high artistic purpose of his tragedies. He joined Jonson in his concern for tragedy as a literary art, and owed him little else.

His relationship to Chapman, whose name properly heads Webster's list, is less general.[9] In his critical position, Webster may seem to be close to Jonson, just as in his language he resembles Shakespeare. But in the essentials of his dramatic structure, in his tragic themes, and even in his apparent intentions in writing tragedy, Webster emulates the explicit, ethically specific manner of such plays as *The Revenge of Bussy D'Ambois* far more than he follows the dramatic but scholarly manner of Jonson or the suggestive, generalized investigation of man and his universe that Shakespeare makes in his tragedies.

To a literate Jacobean such as Webster, Chapman and Jonson had blazed equally worthy trails. They were, in a sense, rival Chams: Chapman, the translator, the serious poet, the successful tragic writer, and Jonson, the literary theorist, the satirist, the successful comic writer. But Chapman was a moralist, and Jonson, for all his satirical depiction of the human scene, was not the purveyor of a full, serious ethical doctrine. Webster, who desired that his writing should be taken seriously, as work of high ethical purpose, seems to have been attracted to Chapman, and to have found in his plays suggestions that materially conditioned the ethical position and the structure of his own tragedies.

"That full and heightened style of Master Chapman" clearly refers to the packed, elevated, sententious, and somewhat obscure language of the tragedies. Although the same adjectives could be applied to it, Webster's language is, in its end result, obviously different, and the allegiance in this area is of small consequence. But Chapman's language, never decorative, cannot be divorced even momentarily from the basic ethical statement of his plays. It is to this ethical substance, which determined the structure of Chapman's tragedies, that Webster appears to have been drawn. The relationship of the dramatists in this area must be considered in detail before the nature, aims, and achievement of Webster's work can be fully understood.[10]

PART ONE

The Tragic Design

CHAPTER ONE

WEBSTER
and CHAPMAN

IN THE FINAL ANALYSIS, the difference between the tragedies of Webster and Chapman is the difference between diamonds and dust. All of Chapman's learned sweat cast no living line; Webster struck fire in every scene. Chapman is admirable, but Webster can be loved as Neander loved Shakespeare. Dryden, however, could use his differentiation between critical love and honor as the basis for setting Shakespeare and Jonson in important opposition; he could have found no such parallel distinction between Webster and Chapman. What difference there is arises from the mettle of the men far more than from their tragic plan or their dramatic techniques. It is a matter of shading, of tone, of the blending of the raw materials of Jacobean tragedy, but it is not, in any sense, a difference in kind, as the difference between Webster and Shakespeare might appear to be. Investigation reveals that Webster is allied to Chapman in many particulars: chiefly in the choice of tragic story, in the use of contemporary references together with a running moral commentary on the contemporary scene, and, most importantly, in the choice of tragic themes which in turn influenced and made similar the techniques by which both dramatists presented the tragic action of their characters.

(13)

"Things like truth"

Chapman chose as materials for his tragedies events of recent French history. What led him to such a choice cannot be fully known,[1] but it is evident that in part he is acting in accordance with an impulse pervasive in Elizabethan and Jacobean drama to use the stage journalistically. Notably in the chronicle histories and some of the domestic tragedies, to a lesser extent in the plays on Roman themes, there is a marked interest in the re-creation of the great events of the past and the sensational events of the present.[2] Chapman's version of French history shows a similar interest in recording the past vividly and truly. It is remarkable how lively and accurate his record is. Grant him the usual necessary license in names and places, his tragedies can still claim fidelity to the historical events they depict, and to a contemporary audience they would have possessed a topical interest long since lost.

Chapman, however, was interested in more than the factual truth of a journalist. He needed materials with which he could conveniently demonstrate general philosophical truth at the same time as he remained faithful to the particular details of recorded history. In the D'Ambois plays, therefore, he selected as his heroes none of the better-known figures of the French court, but an obscure courtier and his fictional brother. Remaining faithful in spirit and in many details to French history, he allowed himself greater freedom in designing the ethical fabric of his story than he would have found had he focused on a more notorious but more limiting protagonist. His subject is "not truth, but things like truth," and he therefore needed a man who approximated the pattern he sought to form, and yet whose career would be sufficiently obscure to permit a poet's augmentation and perfection of details.

The hero of the Byron plays was, of course, better known than Bussy, but popular knowledge of history could come to

Chapman's support and provide overwhelming evidence of the truth of his ethical position. As Parrott says, "Few stories in ancient or modern history give such a poignant and ineffaceable impression of the Nemesis that attends overweening pride."[3] But in telling the story of the Duke of Byron, Chapman was drawing the negative aspects of his morality. In his next tragedy, when he returned to the more difficult depiction of a positive pattern of behavior, he was apparently unable to find in history a man whose career would provide a model for the ethical principles the drama was intended to convey. Clermont D'Ambois, though surrounded with historical personages, was cut from whole cloth.

Besides the somewhat journalistic interest in recent history, and the desire to find factual corroboration for ethical opinion, there is a third possibility that may have led Chapman to his choice of "true" materials. His tragic protagonists, real or imagined, live in no fictive world but in a society which presents them with the major problems of the dramatist's political scene. Chapman was surely as interested in that society as he was in the characters of his heroes. If they are treated with a poet's license, all else, at any rate, is true,[4] and because of this he was able to bring his ethical theory to the test of the world he knew —the only world in which his morality could be of value. Ancient Britain or some Italian never-land would not do. Chapman was compelled to talk about the world in which he lived. His interest in the society of the court, in the government of nations, and in the governors was far from idle. The plays abound in what might not unjustly be called political theory, and they represent Chapman's best thinking about the major issues of his time. Nominally, he is referring to the French political scene, but he repeatedly parallels the French situations with the English. Moreover, his criticism is phrased with such generality as to enable him to move toward absolute considerations, divorced from the special problems of a single country.[5] He thus has a brace of stalking horses to cover his approach to the English scene. Yet, however disguised his political criticism is by its French orientation and by its generality, Chapman remains a dramatist seriously concerned with the problems of his England, and always seeks both to offer explicit counsel to that society and to demonstrate its truth and its force in the lives of his heroes as they move against a background of known fact.

What has been said here of Chapman is equally true of Webster, whose work reflects similar interests and development.[6] *The White Devil* is an intensely contemporary play. It is explicitly concerned with political ethics, and seeks to find some rationale of behavior in a realistically depicted court society. *The Duchess of Malfi* is much broader in its implications. The political background is still present, but now the individuals must face not merely a society but a mortal world—the terror of a dying universe. It is more rich in its philosophical texture, more full in its universal implications than the earlier tragedy. Yet the two plays are conceived in close connection; indeed, *The Duchess of Malfi* is an extension of the meaning of *The White Devil.* Thematically it is a sequel: it stands in precisely the same relation to its sister tragedy as *The Revenge of Bussy D'Ambois* does to its precursor. The important sequential relation between the Chapman plays is obviously not that *The Revenge* continues and concludes the story. There was, in fact, no story to conclude, for the destinies of the minor characters, Bussy being gone, were of no concern to anyone. What is important is that the character of Clermont is an extension, a wiser and fuller version of the "complete man." To present such a man on a comprehensive philosophical basis, Chapman had to leave the recorded events and characters of history, and create a fictional person with whose character he could freely work. It is not, I think, entirely coincidental that Webster does the same thing.

The actual events on which Webster based *The White Devil*

took place about twenty-five years before the tragedy appeared. Vittoria Accoramboni died, probably, on the night of December 22, 1585. It is doubtful that so sensational a story (the events of Webster's tragedy pale beside recorded history) would have entirely receded from men's memories, especially since, in 1601, as Webster was beginning his dramatic career, Virginio Orsini, the Giovanni of the play, was in England as an ambassador from Tuscany. Lucas suggests plausibly enough that Webster had the story by hearsay,[7] and it is reasonable to suppose that if he had heard of it, others also had. It was a story with sufficient contemporary notoriety to pass as historical fact.

The story of the Duchess of Malfi undoubtedly carried with it a more legendary air. The actual Duchess died in 1512, her husband a year later. Her story was told originally by Bandello, passed to Belleforest, and thence to Painter, where Webster found it.[8] There is no reason to suppose that Webster or his audience thought of the story as significantly "true" in any limiting sense. Instead, in his second tragedy Webster was able to achieve a freedom comparable to Chapman's when he departed from the records of history in creating Clermont D'Ambois. Certainly Webster's handling of source material here was freer than in *The White Devil,* and, like Chapman, he created his own pattern of meaning from the materials Painter provided.[9]

Whatever the degree of liberty he took with his sources, Webster never entirely neglected the contemporaneous aspects of his story. For one thing, as Lucas notes, Webster was "far truer to the atmosphere and colour of Renaissance Italy than his contemporaries generally troubled to be. In *The White Devil,* and to a slighter extent in *The Duchess of Malfi,* we have really crossed the Alps; we move in the Amalfi of the House of Aragon, the Rome of Gregory; whereas in *Volpone* or *The Jew of Malta* or *Women beware Women* we seem to have one foot in England still."[10]

A second suggestive circumstance is that, setting aside specific allusion to the Jacobean world, both tragedies call to mind a variety of contemporary or nearly contemporary English scandals, the loves and the death of Mary of Scotland, for instance, or the fate of Lady Arabella Stuart.[11] True or not, the fact that scholars have made plausible cases for such parallels suggests that the tragedies do not exist in a vacuum—that Webster's original audiences could have recognized in his work a world similar to their own.

Finally, the milieu and the atmospheric details of the verse again point toward rather than away from known fact. To take a single important example, the depiction of the court world, both as an actuality on the stage and as a source for imagery, is by no means a fanciful exaggeration. From the last years of Elizabeth's reign, on into the reign of James, the court must have presented to some a spectacle of excess bordering on depravity. There was "hot suit" after courtly rewards in the form of monopolies or offices. The court was filled with flattering parasites seeking to win favor with wealthy nobles. Desperately bizarre behavior and dress became the mode—anything to catch the eye of a patron.[12] Trevelyan notes that "political aspirants were expected to give feasts at £1,000 apiece, present costly hangings, horses and jewellery to all officers and favorites according to their degree, and sit down to dicing-tables where parks and manors were thrown away."[13] This was, in short, a world where Flamineo's pursuit of courtly reward would be understood, and where Brachiano's talent for racketing away "five hundred Crowns at Tennis," and Vittoria's merry heart and "good stomach to a feast" would have seemed in no way unusual. It was a world that existed in fact, and one which, as the satiric writings of the time show, was lashed continually.

It is significant that no other writer of tragedy except Chapman makes use of contemporary story or contemporary detail so spe-

cifically and so constantly as Webster did. Not that Elizabethan
and Jacobean tragic writers were unconcerned with their world.
They realized that tragedy requires more than spectacular sensationalism—that to move men's emotions it must have relevance
to their world. But the journalistic element noted earlier was
never pronounced, and the relevance to the actual world was
shown in other ways than by depicting that world with fidelity to
fact. Tourneur and Marston draw a monstrous caricature of society for satiric purposes. In Shakespearian tragedy the society of
the play bears the same relation to actuality as a symbol does to
the thing symbolized. Webster and Chapman, however, are concerned with verisimilitude, and they appear to be, perhaps for-
tuitously, unique among their fellow dramatists in the deliberate
and continual choice of nearly contemporaneous stories and in
the depiction of a relatively accurate milieu.

"Most sententious Tragedy"

A second important likeness between the dramatists is their perhaps excessive fondness for explicit statement of a general moral
and political nature. Both the omnipresent sententious couplet
and passages offering a more discursive, detailed examination
of the society of the tragedies are so frequent in both dramatists
that neither can completely acquit himself of the charge that he
devised his episodes to provide opportunity for generalized ethical evaluation of court life. Not only does their major attention
seem frequently to be on the sententious statements, with consequent relegation of the action and character to a secondary,
almost illustrative position, but also their conception and development of such scenes are markedly similar in technique.

The opening scenes of *The Revenge of Bussy D'Ambois* and
The Duchess of Malfi provide sufficient evidence of the similarity
of political emphasis and the consequent parallel dramatic devel-

opment. Chapman's play opens with a conversation between
two courtiers, Baligny and Revel, in which the present state of
the French court is compared unfavorably with the glories of the
past, when there could be observed

> Rule in more regular motion: things most lawful
> Were once most royal; kings sought common good,
> Men's manly liberties, though ne'er so mean,
> And had their own swing so more free, and more.
> But when pride enter'd them, and rule by power,
> All brows that smil'd beneath them, frown'd; hearts griev'd
> By imitation; virtue quite was vanish'd,
> And all men studied self-love, fraud, and vice;
> Then no man could be good but he was punish'd:
> Tyrants being still more fearful of the good
> Than of the bad; their subjects' virtues ever
> Manag'd with curbs and dangers, and esteem'd
> As shadows and detractions to their own.
>
> (I, i, 19)

As the court enters, the two pass to *sotto voce* comments on the
Guise, Monsieur, and Clermont—comments which stress their
varied abilities as servants of their king. This commentary, while
helping to define the characters, serves more importantly to
establish the norm of virtuous government against which all
characters and events can be measured. Clermont, by the light
of the commentary, is seen as an exemplary courtier; Baligny,
who here preaches order and openness and honesty in government, is later discovered to be a Machiavel, masking his treachery
with the best counsel.

The first scene of *The Duchess of Malfi* is exactly similar in
method. Antonio has just returned to Italy from the French
court, and at Delio's request describes the virtues displayed by
the French king in purging the court of sycophants and in gath-
ering only honest advisers about him. The passage stresses the
duties of courtiers in advising their king.[14] Although the specifi-

cally political subject matter is not so central to *The Duchess of Malfi* as to *The White Devil,* if the passage is read with the earlier tragedy in mind it can be seen that Webster and Chapman share a community of interest in such topics. Certainly *The White Devil* is concerned almost entirely with the relation of courtier to prince, a theme which, having been fully treated there, is relegated to a less conspicuous place in the main action of *The Duchess of Malfi.* Yet, as with Chapman, the opening discussion does provide a kind of norm by which the immediately succeeding episodes can be judged.

Antonio's discourse is followed by Bosola's entrance, his meeting with the Cardinal, and his railing exposition of the evils that come from dependency on such a master as the Cardinal. And Webster is soon to show the Machiavels of the play, setting Bosola in the Duchess' household as a spy, much as Baligny is revealed as a spy in *The Revenge of Bussy D'Ambois.*

Beyond this—and again the parallel with Chapman is striking— when the scene swells with the entrance of Ferdinand and his courtiers, Delio and Antonio stand to one side and comment descriptively on the Aragonian brothers, stressing their unethical behavior as responsible men of affairs. The scene is entirely reminiscent of the dialogue between Baligny and Revel in Chapman's tragedy.

Demonstration of such thematic and technical similarities between the dramatists could be extended indefinitely, but such parallels are at best circumstantial indications of more important relationships. Two matters stand out as of particular concern: first, the similarity of the central conflict in each dramatist; and second, the resultant similarity of techniques of characterization.

The Tragedy of the Complete Man

The D'Ambois and the Byron plays are conceived in the tradition of the Renaissance courtesy books: they endeavor to establish the pattern of a noble man, who not only is the perfect courtier but also has perfected within himself the fullest capabilities of the human spirit. The D'Ambois brothers are clearly designed to be copied. *The Revenge of Bussy D'Ambois* is described by Chapman as an "excitation to heroical life," and, in the dedication to the play, tragedy is defined in terms of its ethical statement: "material instruction, elegant and sententious excitation to virtue, and deflection from her contrary, being the soul, limbs, and limits of an authentical tragedy." In the sense here defined, Chapman's tragedies are undoubtedly "authentical." It is not merely that Chapman draws a moral from a melodrama. He attempts to weave the entire tragic fabric so as to portray the elements of the heroic life, a life which will provide a pattern worthy of emulation, or, as with the Duke of Byron, a pattern which can serve as a warning of the snares in which greatness is liable to be entangled.

The elements in the pattern of the noble man were chosen in accordance with an austere but positive ethical theory based on a combination of Christian and stoic ethics.[15] The hero was modeled after the stoic philosopher, the man who had realized his potential inner strength to a degree where he was contemptuous of the rewards of Fortune, ready for death, and therefore able through the strength of his character to endure any evil. He was perfect—in Chapman's phrase, "a complete man."[16] His perfection, in turn, gave rise to the unique consistency of his actions. Of supreme importance to the complete man is the integrity of his personality. He must sometimes struggle to preserve this core of his identity, but more frequently in Chapman he must continually assert it. Such assertion of his fundamental *virtù* is his rule of life; by it he keeps "decorum" in Cicero's sense.[17] Only by maintaining this consistency of character can the hero triumph over the evils which seek to destroy him.

Evil in Chapman's tragedies, though not so carefully schematized as the pattern of heroic good, is associated mainly with the principles of Machiavelli. The Machiavellism of the Jacobean dramatists, whether by design, ignorance of the original, or the general drifting distortion of stage tradition, bore little resemblance to its source. Chapman perhaps kept better faith than most with his original, for his Machiavels operated in a sphere of distinctly political activity, but, like many of his contemporaries, he seems to have felt that they were incarnations of a kind of abstract evil. They possess no integrity whatever. In sharp contrast to the hero, they are entirely venal. Their spirit is malignant, their methods labyrinthine and treacherous, their vengeance horrible, and their motivation frequently only a stark joy of doing evil. They work against the protagonist by attacking his greatest strength, the core of his individuality. This they do in two ways, by direct oppression, or by laying such temptations in the hero's path that he will depart from the principle of decorum and prove false to himself.

In *Bussy D'Ambois,* evil attacks directly. Bussy's assertion of his *virtù* is challenged at every turn. As an individual he is frequently in opposition to the entire social structure in which he moves—D'Ambois against the world. There is no question of his being tempted out of the course which his self-assertion has set for him. He must be attacked directly, his strength destroyed by murder. The Duke of Byron, on the contrary, need not be crushed. He is tempted by flattering appeals to his sense of his own greatness, and he succumbs. The Machiavels claim him for their own. The great courtier becomes a traitor, hiding his treason behind the façade of his former magnificence, and the duplicity destroys him. Although Chapman does not condone Byron's treason, he makes it apparent, in the final scenes of *The Tragedy of Charles Duke of Byron,* that Byron's mere admission of treason would be sufficient to restore him partially to virtue, and that his persistent clinging to his remembered greatness amounts to insanity. Byron's greatest crime is not treason but hypocrisy. Evil, working from within, has caused him to forsake the principles of decorum, not by asserting that he is good when in actuality he is evil, but by maintaining that he is something other than what he essentially is, be it good or evil.

Thus the large design of Chapman's tragedies is established by the basic conflict of the Senecal man and the Machiavel. The conflict is revealed explicitly in *The Revenge of Bussy D'Ambois* in a dialogue between the Guise and the King. The Guise is protesting the arrest of the hero, Clermont D'Ambois, and concludes a lengthy speech in his praise by saying:

> *Guise:* In short, this Senecal man is found in him,
>   He may with heaven's immortal powers compare,
>   To whom the day and fortune equal are;
>   Come fair or foul, whatever chance can fall,
>   Fix'd in himself, he still is one to all. . . .
> *Henry:* And apprehend I this man for a traitor?
> *Guise:* These are your Machiavellian villains,
>   Your bastard Teucers, that, their mischiefs done,
>   Run to your shield for shelter, Cacusses
>   That cut their too large murderous thieveries
>   To their dens' length still: woe be to that state
>   Where treachery guards, and ruin makes men great!
>   (IV, iv, 42, 54)

Here is the design in its bare essentials, brought to the ethical focus of a conflict of doctrines: the teachings of Machiavelli and of Seneca as they were understood or utilized in Jacobean England.[18]

As the foregoing quotation suggests, this basic ethical structure created dramatic problems which were not easily solved. The Senecal hero, in this scheme of things, is not readily brought into the action of the drama. Clermont D'Ambois, fixed in himself, is beset by the activity of the Machiavels who, through no fault of his, seek his downfall. He is a relatively passive figure. In *The Revenge of Bussy D'Ambois,* the Machiavels alone, because of their onslaughts on the *virtù* of the tragic hero, keep the drama on the move. The hero is forced into a position which, throughout most of the tragedy, is passive, defensive of his essential integrity, and resistant to change.

This is not to say that in Jacobean tragedy the forces of evil *necessarily* dominate the action of the play. Dramatic action may be defined as the movement of a character toward the realization of a goal which he has consciously or subconsciously established as of supreme importance. Such movement must be realized in terms of human behavior, but action is distinct from activity in that it is purposive, controlled, and progressive, providing a measure for the direction and velocity of all activity. In this sense, each character in a drama will be provided with an "action," a goal toward which he moves and directs his activity. It is obvious, however, that the dramatic action of a play is not a cluttered complex of conflicting subsidiary actions. All actions in a well-written play will come into focus around the principal drive of the central character, either supporting it, opposing it, or generalizing it by a parallel relationship. The evildoers may have a greater share of activity, and therefore appear more active than the heroes, but they do not necessarily have a more significant action. The goal of a dramatic action may well be conceived as the attainment of a state of being, an effort to understand the reasons for suffering, or perhaps a struggle to maintain integrity of spirit.

The defensive passivity of the Jacobean tragic hero meant, however, that he could not control the activity of the play, but would be brought into the focal position only as a target for the slings and arrows of the antagonists. Any attempt to combat evil meant that he would take the law into his own hands, leaving himself vulnerable to the contamination of evil, and causing him to risk loss of the integrity of self so essential to the strength of the good. His place, logically, was to suffer, and his way to triumph was by quietly opposing to evil the impregnable strength of his *virtù*. It is implicit in the Jacobean tragic pattern that the hero is to demonstrate the validity of his ethical position by a steadfast refusal to take arms against trouble. But demonstration of ethical precept is not fully drama. Too readily it becomes a substitute for characterization. The core of the technical problem for these dramatists was how to reveal the character of the hero in significant dramatic action.

Chapman's Tragic Action

Chapman's solution of the problem of how to reveal dramatically the character of the inactive hero is not especially satisfactory. But what, after all, could be done with a hero who self-consciously (and somewhat priggishly) placed the highest value on the supreme consistency of his character. "The complete man" is the impregnable man, "all in all sufficient"; his is "the noble nature . . . passion could not shake," the man so perfect that he cannot be benefited by a change in character. He is "complete" precisely because he does *not* change. His failure to show development during the course of the drama is, in fact, part of his *virtu,* for he was endowed with stoic fortitude as his very birthright. His triumph lies in maintaining himself as he essentially is, whatever the caprices of fortune.

Bussy D'Ambois reveals clearly that an ethical scheme which dispenses with developing character in the interest of presenting a moral model creates difficulties for the dramatist. The significant action is minimal, the activity irrelevant to the theme and therefore frequently melodramatic. Stubbornly the theme refuses to incorporate with the events of the story in such a way as to organize its random activity into a pattern of meaningful dramatic action. Although he is intended to represent the "complete man," an incarnation of *noblesse* in its natural state, Bussy does nothing to reveal his *virtu*. He is talked about, his *virtù* is endlessly extolled, but he passes through the play on parade. Nowhere is the "complete man" revealed in purposive action, either aggressive or defensive. He does not suffer; he does not even have to struggle to maintain his individuality. Like Tamburlaine's, his strength is so great that evil cannot touch him. Nor does he act against evil in any real way. Instead, as Dryden noted, he huffs and fights;[19] he is upstairs, downstairs, and in my lady's chamber. But his activity is meaningless. The D'Ambois of the story is quite distinct from the D'Ambois of the theme, and it is significant that an understanding of him in the latter capacity comes almost entirely from explicit ethical description, not from the action of the play.

The Conspiracy and Tragedy of Charles Duke of Byron is Chapman's ten-act study of the man who, though he gives every appearance of *virtù,* lacks the essential integration of personality that makes him not only great but good. As the play opens, he is the most magnificent of men in the kingdom. He says of himself,

> I stand on change,
> And shall dissolve in changing;
> (I, ii, 27)

meaning that any alteration of his personal worth will result in dissolution of his total being. His only possible direction is upward: "'Tis immortality to die aspiring," he says; he must seek continually for what is "high and right." His desire is for more of the glory he already has, a continuing expansion of the personality analogous to Tamburlaine's expansion of his power over the countries on his line of march. But Byron, unlike Tamburlaine, reaches a limit. He can rise no higher and not be greater than the king. There is thus established a conflict between loyalty to the king and loyalty to himself. Byron, swerving from his loyalty to the king, breaks his neck on ambition's vaulting horse. Yet Byron is no Macbeth, destroyed in his self-awareness. In the end, when he is on the scaffold, he reveals no characteristic that he has not shown at the outset. Chapman, in fact, makes a fine ironic point out of Byron's steadfast refusal to admit his guilt. Unshaken, he asserts his claims to *virtù,* and makes heroic denial of change in his personality:

> You have not done
> Like a good Justice, and one that knew
> He sat upon the precious blood of virtue; . . .
> You have condemn'd me, my Lord Chancellor,
> But God acquits me. . . .
> (V, iii, 92, 98)

In a frenzy he recalls the height of his glory at the siege of Amiens,

> Where, cover'd all in showers of shot and fire,
> I seem'd to all men's eyes a fighting flame
> With bullets cut in fashion of a man,
> A sacrifice to valour. . . .
> (V, iii, 166)

Such remembered facts, the audience realizes, are present illusions, and therefore ironic in their irrelevance. But Byron sees no irony in his behavior. He is blinded by his conception of his own glory, and his frenzy on the scaffold results from unwillingness to admit that his greatness has actually dissolved through change.

There is to be no ambiguity in Byron's final appearances. His heroics are not to dazzle the audience into forgetting his guilt. Characteristically, Chapman falls back on explicit statement to make his emphasis clear. Two courtiers sum up the ultimate impression of Byron's character:

> Oh of what contraries consists a man!
> Of what impossible mixtures! Vice and virtue,

> Corruption, and eternness, at one time,
> And in one subject, let together loose!
> We have not any strength but weakens us,
> No greatness but doth crush us into air. . . .
>
> O Virtue, thou art now far worse than Fortune; . . .
> Thy powers are shadows, and thy comfort, dreams. . . .
>
> O real Goodness, if thou be a power,
> And not a word alone, in human uses,
> Appear out of this angry conflagration,
> Where this great captain, thy late temple, burns,
> And turn his vicious fury to thy flame
> From all earth's hopes mere gilded with thy fame: . . .
>
> (V, iii, 189, 210)

In the end, his mind framed to stoical renunciation of the world, Byron supplements these ethical choristers with observations admitting his own guilt.

> Farewell world!
> He is at no end of his actions blest
> Whose ends will make him greatest, and not best.
>
> (V, iv, 143)

And again,

> Fall on your knees then, statists, ere ye fall,
> That you may rise again: knees bent too late,
> Stick you in earth like statues: see in me
> How you are pour'd down from your clearest heavens;
> Fall lower yet, mix'd with th' unmoved centre,
> That your own shadows may no longer mock ye.
>
> (V, iv, 253)

But with three more lines the play is over, and it is too late for such admission to be considered truly a development or even a recognition of change in character. Byron simply draws the moral of his own story; his admission is a dramatist's device, not a revelation of the inner man.

Although Byron disintegrates under the attack of evil, he is never seen as a man maturing through suffering. In his own eyes he does not change, and therefore he never questions or seeks to understand himself. To an audience, therefore, his suffering is not of especial importance. He is viewed, rather, in an ironic perspective that makes him little more than an example of the ethical conclusions of the dramatist. Chapman uses him as a sinful object lesson for his generalized commentary on the human scheme; he does not study the terrifying changes which sin effects in the man. Indeed, so pervasive is the irony of Byron's position in the end that only his belief in his consistency leaves him a shred of heroism and prevents his becoming foolishly pitiable.

In the Byron plays, Chapman is stating that a man who, through excess of *virtù,* aspires to become a law unto himself must fall, a tree too lofty for its roots. This position is apparently a revaluation of the ethical conclusions of *Bussy D'Ambois,* whose hero, also a law to himself, was not quite convincing as a pattern of heroic life. In *The Revenge of Bussy D'Ambois,* Chapman makes a further revision of opinion about the nature of the "complete man," finding him in the person of Bussy's brother Clermont to be the Christian stoic. Again the characteristic ethical structure is evident, and again Chapman is less interested in what his hero is than in what he represents. He is concerned not with spiritual revelation but with general considerations of man's external relation to the world.[20]

Clermont D'Ambois, like Hamlet, is not the ideal revenger, for he is a contemplative rather than an active man. The necessity for revenge, however, involves Clermont in no such dilemma as Hamlet's. His plans are carefully laid; they are honorable, and he is willing to abide their maturing. For him, yielding to stealth or to blind butcher's fury is inconceivable. It is a sin against his *virtù.* Urged to take immediate revenge, he refuses, and adds,

> Nor can we call it virtue that proceeds
> From vicious fury. I repent . . .
> That e'er I yielded to revenge his [Bussy's] murder.
> All worthy men should ever bring their blood
> To bear all ill, not to be wreak'd with good:
> Do ill for no ill; never private cause
> Should take on it the part of public laws.
>   (III, ii, 108, 116)

He insists that the revenge shall be effected through a gentleman's
channels, by means of a properly delivered challenge and a duel.
When Montsurry, Bussy's murderer, refuses to accept the challenge, Clermont is content to wait until time will permit the duel
to take place. Clermont always is in the right. If not the ideal
revenger, he is the ideal man, and, since the actual revenge is
the major topic only in the first and the fifth acts, the greater part
of the play is concerned with demonstrating in what ways he is
an exemplar of heroic *virtù*.

Clermont's particular *virtù* is revealed by his refusal to yield
to the temptation of ambition. Birth, place, public honor are
unattractive to him. The man who tries to rise in worldly spheres
is a defier of God's plan, and in some measure a fool.

> God hath the whole world perfect made and free,
> His parts to th' use of th' All; men then that be
> Parts of that All, must, as the general sway
> Of that importeth, willingly obey
> In everything without their power to change.
> He that, unpleas'd to hold his place, will range,
> Can in no other be contain'd that's fit,
> And so resisting th' All, is crush'd with it.
>   (III, iv, 58)

It is godlike for a man to confine "freely his whole powers in his
proper part," to accept his lot, to seek to "join himself with th'
Universe," and, in Chapman's image, "go on round as it." His
acceptance of God's plan enables Clermont to rely completely

upon himself. Whatever Fortune deals out, be it what the world calls good or bad, he accepts with equanimity. Indeed, he brags of this composure, and when he is asked how one learns to love bad like the good, replies,

> To love nothing outward,
> Or not within our own powers to command;
> And so being sure of everything we love,
> Who cares to lose the rest? If any man
> Would neither live nor die in his free choice,
> But as he sees necessity will have it
> (Which if he would resist, he strives in vain)
> What can come near him, that he doth not will,
> And if in worst events his will be done,
> How can the best be better? All is one.
>
> (IV, v, 4)

In such a deterministic scheme, no action is possible. No desire, no goal can be established, since a man can want nothing except the knowledge of his personal integrity. No suffering is conceivable, since the hero's stoical contempt for both external good and evil provides him with enduring anodyne. No change in character is necessary, since perfection has already been achieved. Clermont D'Ambois, in short, is the model of the passive hero.[21]

The effects on the play are, of course, severe, for it is to display the stoical qualities of his hero that Chapman devises the incidents of his tragedy. The Senecal man need only be tested in his philosophical position, and, as a result, conflict is minimized, activity is negligible, and the line of dramatic action is tenuous. Continually, the play is stopped to allow for what Chapman calls "virtuous digressions," intended to elaborate the niceties of Clermont's behavior. The character is thus presented by descriptive means rather than by action. The ethical points are explicitly made, and the character behaves in illustration of the precept. For Chapman, the moral philosophy is all.

There never was a work written for the professional stage that made fewer concessions to the audience than *The Revenge of Bussy D'Ambois*. *Irene* is a Christmas pantomime beside it. Unquestionably it is a lamentable drama, but it is also, ironically enough, Chapman's best tragedy. It has none of the absurdity that arises from the incompatibility of theme and fable in *Bussy D'Ambois*. Nor is it, for all the tenuousness of its plot, so vapid a drama as the ten-act *Conspiracy and Tragedy of Charles Duke of Byron*. Moreover, it has at least the signal virtue of doing what it sets out to do firmly and with dispatch. No time is wasted on sensational events or on comic interludes.[22] And though the poverty of incident makes the play dull on the stage or in the study, it is clear that Chapman has refused to compromise with his original intentions by introducing irrelevant melodrama. The language is "full and heightened," but it is sometimes so heightened as to be barbarously obscure, so full as to be, in the theater, syntactically impenetrable. Yet again, since Chapman elsewhere displays his ability to write good stage verse, the choice of a dialogue style must have been deliberate. Chapman —this much at least must be said for him—had the solid virtue of knowing what he was up to. He had the courage of his own dullness.

Grant him, too, the virtues of intensity and of raising problems of contemporary interest. His moral explication, albeit long-winded, is sustained throughout the five acts. This is partly the result of his sinewy verse, but more the result of the powers of his mind to come to grips with his material, and to survey and explicate it thoroughly. The play is an admirable intellectual enterprise. Furthermore, Chapman was undoubtedly aware that he was contributing an interpretation of some of the major ethical and philosophical problems of the time. He elected to phrase this discussion in terms of nearly contemporary events, the history of France within the range of men's memories. In addition, so far as he could or dared, he extended his consideration of the political and ethical worlds, both by analogy and direct reference, to England. Unquestionably, Chapman's plays must have seemed to thoughtful listeners or readers to be major attempts to solve certain of their problems. This was their world; these were, in a measure, their questions. They must have admired Chapman for his straightforward, honest, highly serious attempt to talk about the contemporary world.

Such at least were some of the qualities of "Master Chapman" that caused Webster to be drawn to him when, after a period of apprentice hack work, he undertook to create a tragedy in his own right. *The White Devil* displays the same interest in the contemporary world and its problems, the same leaning toward explicit ethical generality, the same refusal to reveal the inner world of spirit in the characters, the same presentation of character in terms of precept and example rather than by depicting growth through suffering—in short, the same ethical structure as in the D'Ambois and Byron plays. The verbal borrowings tell only a part of Webster's conception of tragedy, and the allegiance to Shakespeare they suggest is superficial. Far more important is Webster's explicit statement of his major dependence on the tragedies of Chapman, and, in accordance with his own suggestion, it is "by their light" that *The White Devil* and *The Duchess of Malfi* must be read.

CHAPTER TWO # W<small>EBSTER'S</small>
TRAGIC ACTION

THE MORAL PHILOSOPHY of Chapman was not quite "all" for Webster. This, though a fortunate fact, does not seem to have arisen from any sense on Webster's part of the shortcomings of Chapman's tragic scheme, for he comes as close to it as he can. The ground plan for his tragedy is markedly similar to that sketched in the previous chapter for Chapman. *The White Devil* and *The Duchess of Malfi* are both constructed around the conflict of the Senecan protagonist with the Machiavellian antagonist. At the death of each of the central characters, the stoical resolution sounds clearly. The Duchess welcomes death as a gift, the best her brothers can give her. Bosola admits his death is pain, but sees that in it there is only good. Vittoria feels nothing but contempt for her murderers and the death they bring, and Flamineo speaks for both himself and his sister when he says,

> "This busy trade of life appears most vain,
> "Since rest breeds rest, where all seek pain by pain.
>   (*WD,* V, vi, 273)

Opposed to the stoical protagonists are again the Machiavels and, as in Chapman, it is Machiavellism with a distinct political orientation. The Machiavels are the devious, subtle court politicians, the dukes and their sycophants, who find no villainy too unscrupulous for their objectives, who sometimes are to be sus-

(35)

pected of valuing the means of villainy over the ends. Flamineo (who like Bosola is part Machiavel, part stoic[1]) describes the Machiavels with a kind of delight that suggests a connoisseur's allegiance to their ways:

> Those are found weighty strokes which come from th' hand,
> But those are killing strokes which come from th' head.
> O the rare tricks of a Machivillian!
> He doth not come like a gross plodding slave
> And buffet you to death: No, my quaint knave—
> He tickles you to death; makes you die laughing;
> As if you had swallow'd down a pound of saffron.
> You see the feat—'tis practis'd in a trice—
> To teach Court-honesty it jumps on Ice.
>
> (V, iii, 194)

The audience is provided with many examples of the artistry of these murderers: Ferdinand's delight in torturing his sister by degrees, Francisco's involved method of poisoning Brachiano, Vittoria's dream of the yew tree, and Bosola's intelligencing. Most vivid, perhaps, is Lodovico's morbid delight in his butcher's artistry:

> I do glory yet,
> That I can call this act mine own: For my part,
> The rack, the gallows, and the torturing wheel
> Shall be but sound sleeps to me, here's my rest—
> "I limn'd this night-piece and it was my best.
>
> (V, vi, 295)

Here again Jacobean stoicism, the contempt for suffering, the willingness to take evil as a good, is matched with Jacobean Machiavellism, the delight in evil, frequently with the sense that the only "good" is evil. Once more the conflict is used as a basis for setting forth a definite ethical scheme, which apparently was intended in some measure as a solution to contemporary problems.

In Websterian tragedy there is less concern for creating positive models of behavior than there is in the tragedies of Chapman. The Duchess speaks of Antonio as a "complete man,"[2] and Bosola's praise of him, in Act III, scene i, as a man who has risen through his virtues rather than by his pedigree, has a basis in demonstrated fact. Marcello in *The White Devil* has something of this quality, too. Yet neither, obviously, has anything like the force of Bussy or Clermont. The Duchess is the only real possibility of an ethical model, but her potential weakness of character makes her a figure altogether foreign to the context of a Chapman play.

Webster manages to convey, however, the sense of precept and example that Chapman's tragedies suggest. The explicit general commentary forces much, perhaps all, of his action and therefore most of his characters into an exemplary relationship to his themes. Particularly, he dwells on what might be termed negative models, men whose lives are a pattern to be avoided. Antonio's commentary on the Cardinal and Ferdinand has already been cited.[3] *The White Devil's* parallel set of villains, Brachiano, Zanche, and many others, provide additional instances. Some ambiguity attaches itself to an audience's moral attitude toward Bosola, Flamineo, Vittoria, and even the Duchess. But there is nothing ambiguous about the others. They are interpreted throughout with explicit ethical emphasis. They are the ones to whom Antonio has reference when he says, dying, "Let my Son, fly the Courts of Princes," and their evil is clearly defined throughout by a running commentary on their true natures.

In the ambiguous evaluation of Vittoria, the Duchess, Flamineo, and Bosola, however, the first essential difference between the dramatists can be noted. Chapman tends to make a sharp division between the good and the evil factions, for he simplifies character in just such a way as he simplifies the action of his stories. With Webster the leading figures are more complicated, because Machiavellian and Senecan qualities combine in the same person: Flamineo is in his actions for Brachiano a Machiavel; yet he is also a man who distrusts worldly possessions and honors, a man who knows the folly of being anything less than his own master. His dying words epitomize the Senecan element in Websterian tragedy:

> "We cease to grieve, cease to be fortune's slaves,
> "Nay cease to die by dying.
>
> (V, vi, 252)

Bosola also combines the two doctrines, and with Flamineo-like callousness, holds the world, himself included, in such stoical contempt that any activity, however degrading, is acceptable. The main basis of Vittoria's action is stoical, but in the early part of the play she is a Machiavel. The Duchess, although she is clearly not allied with Machiavellism, unless it be in the secrecy of her marriage, displays some of the personality traits of the Machiavel, notably a tendency to lose her hold on the identifying *virtù* that makes her a great woman.

The resultant impression of good and evil confounded, especially at the end of *The Duchess of Malfi,* when the dying speeches of all the Machiavels are given a stoical cast, is on the whole foreign to Chapman. In drawing the character of Byron, he most clearly anticipated Webster's practice, but Byron tends to be an oscillation between the Senecan and Machiavellian factions rather than a mixture of the two. Byron is now good, now evil; he never occasions such a puzzling moral response as do Vittoria and Bosola. The villain-hero is Webster's stock in trade,[4] and his effect on the characterization and the ethical structure of the tragedies is distinctive.

"Integrity of life"

The intermingling of Senecanism and Machiavellism in the central figures undeniably gives to Webster's characters a complexity

that suggests the profound studies of good and evil of Shakespearian tragedy, but Webster's method of creating character is
not that of Shakespeare. Websterian tragedy can be fully com-
prehended only when it is understood that development of character, in the sense that Shakespeare's heroes change and grow,
is not a central element. If Shakespeare's tragedy be conceived
as a vortex, centering the moral universe in the suffering soul of
an individual, then Webster's may be likened to a framed general
action, like a stage panorama, which makes its most significant
revelations through the presentation of man's relations to man.
Webster studies not men as individuals with inherent differences,
but mankind, children of Goodman Adam, strikingly alike, shar-
ing innate characteristics. Shakespearian tragedy is individual,
with a suggested generality of application; Websterian tragedy
is broadly social, with individuals serving as normative examples
of Webster's conception of life. In this it is like the tragedy of
Chapman. And it is like Chapman's, further, in that it is not a
record of spiritual growth through suffering but of tenacious
resistance to oppression.

Webster's tragedy is strikingly different from both Chapman's
and Shakespeare's because, in the large view, no one character
stands out as spiritually most significant: it might almost be said
that Websterian tragedy has no tragic hero. For Webster, a
character is important not in terms of the wellsprings of his
thoughts and actions, but in terms of his relationships, the effects
of his thoughts and actions on his fellow men. Shakespeare's
tragedies were born of splendid, unwavering acceptance of
humanity. Chapman's offer an austere yet noble pattern of
conduct to an ignoble world. Webster's are didactic, satiric,
harshly critical of man's society. Their core is the condition of
that society, not the growth of the human spirit, and character
is important not in itself but with respect to the relationships
which are a formative part of an excoriate world.

To say that Webster's characters do not develop is not to say
that they are nothing more than Chapman's shadow puppets of
color and line. As they struggle against oppression, they achieve
a depth and a dramatic vitality unknown to Chapman. Webster
made the oppressive forces more potent than the straw men who
oppose Bussy D'Ambois, and therefore made the struggle more
desperate and dramatically more affecting. Yet it is idle to seek
in Websterian tragedy for a pattern based on "that development
of human souls for good or evil, which is Shakespeare's especial
power." The Websterian characters, Bosola included, are in the
end what they were at the outset. The naturally evil men and
women remain evil; the good remain good. The more heroic
are completely, even stubbornly, consistent. It is a matter of
pride with them that misfortune does not change them. Their
entire struggle—the struggle which makes them alive on the
stage—is to keep themselves as they are, essentially.

A phrase that Webster uses will serve to designate the consistency to self which his characters reveal. It is found significantly in the last two lines of *The Duchess of Malfi.* It is the
summing-up. Delio says,

> *"Integrity of life, is fame's best friend,*
> *Which nobly (beyond Death) shall crown the end.*

Integrity of life is the *virtù* of Websterian character. In its context the phrase is applied to an action which would traditionally
be judged "good," but it has a more fundamental application.
To Webster, integrity of life cuts across the traditional evaluative
divisions of good and evil, and proves, in the final synthesis, to
be the sole standard of positive ethical judgment in the tragedies.

It is true that Webster makes use of traditional standards of
moral evaluation in delineating his characters. But, for him,
these standards shift alarmingly; the usual distinctions between
good and evil become inadequate for a true picture of life and

are finally passed over. Man's world, as Webster sees it, is a "deep pit of darkness," and mankind is "womanish and fearful" in the shadow of the pit. The causes of the fear are many, but chief among them are *oppression* and *mortality*. Oppression is the social cause: man's inhumanity to man, the destruction of the individual by society, represented in the tragedies by a corrupt court of law, perhaps, or the vicious social system where able men are forced to sycophancy to obtain rewards from their prince. Mortality is the natural cause. It too means destruction —the decay of the living body by disease and the destruction of the dead flesh by worms and the festering rot of the churchyard.

Whether Webster consistently saw these causes as coequal is not clear. He is explicitly concerned with both throughout his tragedies, but toward the end of *The Duchess of Malfi* there is a shift in balance. It appears that he saw natural mortality, finally, as underlying all things, enveloping and eventually destroying even social oppression in its individual manifestations. At times it seems possible to interpret oppression as symbolic of the processes of mortality, as in the fourth act of *The Duchess of Malfi*. However this may be, death is clearly the end of a "long war." Man, after a few years of struggle, comes to nothing. Whatever his degree of magnificence, whether he adhered to the traditional principles of good or indulged in bizarre evils, he comes inevitably to dust. And the dust has no meaning:

> *Of what is't fools make such vain keeping?*
> *Sin their conception, their birth, weeping:*
> *Their life, a general mist of error,*
> *Their death, a hideous storm of terror—*
>
> (*DM*, IV, ii, 188)

As the great dirge suggests, the common bond between men is their mortality. It spreads through the world, meshing man with man, making their differences insignificant, defeating good and evil alike. The central question of the tragedies is not, therefore,

What is good and what is evil, but What is the use of life? *Why should man have any life at all if life means only destruction?*

In the "pit of darkness" all men worthy of the name must face the question. There is a positive quality in these people, something in the fact of their having life, that leads them to this necessity. Some are animals, spawn of the pit, the Zanches and Julias, who do not sense the question. Some are cowards, the Cariolas, who cannot face the unrelenting fact. Some are hypocrites, like Monticelso, Francisco, and notably the Aragonian brothers, who avoid seeing the somber truth by clinging to hypocritical masks of temporal justice and worldly honor. Finally, there are the defiant ones, the great ones, who face the question squarely and spit back not an answer but an assertion that while they live they will be what they are, whether it be good or evil. As they were born, so they will die, and, short of death, no force of man or nature can change them. While they have conscious will, they must "Defy the worst of fate; not fear to bleed."

This defiance, this holding true to one's essential nature, whatever it may be, is integrity of life. Its maintenance, by the overcoming of womanish fears, and the assertion of self in the face of mortality and oppression that seek to destroy the essential nature of man, is the source of struggle in the tragedies. Introspection has no place, nor has hesitation, recanting penitence, or seeking of other than worldly happiness. The maintenance of integrity is a positive action, for it means following the dictates of one's nature, against the tides of society if need be, until the wave of opposition that has been generated by that action brings overwhelming destruction.

It is important, therefore, that the great individuals of Websters' tragedies do not change. If they did, the one positive value in the world, the only measure of man, would prove chimerical, and man would be consigned forever to the womanish fears of the pit. Inner struggle and development have no place in the Websterian view of life. They lead nowhere, for death is all. No regeneration through suffering is possible.

In depicting such a situation, Webster studies not individuality as it relates to good and evil in the moral universe, but individualism as it rebels against the limiting bonds of the flesh. The pattern of Websterian tragedy is this. The hideous norms of the world are mortality and oppression. An individual struggles to escape the laws of the norm, is caught, falls back, and is reabsorbed in the general level. This pattern of aberrational struggle and defeat continually recurs. It is a law of man's nature and his world. Thus the most individualistic action becomes horribly typical. Even the great ones cannot escape, but are trapped and destroyed, as surely as the weak must perish.

The result, so far as this pattern affects the creation of character, is that the people in *The White Devil* and *The Duchess of Malfi* become representative rather than individual and are viewed in terms of their outward aspects rather than their inner natures. Once their fundamental identities are established, their course of action, rebellious, oppressive, or merely yielding, becomes more important than their motives. It is the fight, not the character of the fighter, that reveals most about the tragic structure of the world. For this reason, although the Duchess is undeniably an individual and suffers martyrdom because she insisted on remaining an individual, she does not possess the inner reality of a Shakespearian tragic hero. The audience sees in her only what the people on the stage see, and is rarely permitted to look deeper. Her problem is to face the world with dignity, and her accomplishment is that she manages, despite the powers of darkness which attack her, to maintain and assert her integrity as she dies. But, except for a few moments when her fight against madness necessarily brings the inner struggle to the surface, the audience sees not the struggle itself but the results of the struggle. And it is the results which are important. For the fourth act of *The Duchess of Malfi* is more than the record of an individual's martyrdom. It is a testing ground of the finest human spirit, Webster's attempt to prove for all men the value in tenacious resistance to destruction. As such, it becomes a representative or symbolic action in which the individual, though important, is subordinated to a general conception of the condition of human life.

The Individual in the Type

Webster's concentration on the outer aspects of his people is further demonstrated by an analysis of the technical means which he used to depict character. In Shakespearian tragedy, the inner being of a tragic hero is revealed through soliloquy, through individuality of behavior, and through gradual exploration of the motives for action. An analysis of the kind of revelation which Webster makes by these means will emphasize the essentially different intentions of the two dramatists.

The Soliloquy

Far from serving to reveal inner spiritual reality, the Websterian soliloquy is used only to assist the development of plot by clarifying certain obscurities. The few soliloquies in *The White Devil* are used to convey information to the audience which otherwise might not be apparent: that Brachiano's tears for Isabella are hypocritical, or that Francisco has determined on revenge, despite his remarks to the contrary. These are explanatory rather than revelatory, serving to elucidate ambiguous external action. The only soliloquy in *The White Devil* that seems to be put to a more than expository use is given to Flamineo. At the sight of his mother's insanity, he is moved to exclaim, in tones of wondering incomprehension,

> I have a strange thing in me, to th' which
> I cannot give a name without it be
> Compassion.
>   (V, iv, 107)

But the "strange" feeling is laid aside, and what follows is descriptive rather than dramatic:

>   I have liv'd
> Riotously ill, like some that live in Court.
> And sometimes, when my face was full of smiles,
> Have felt the mace of conscience in my breast.
> Oft gay and honour'd robes those tortures try,
> "We think cag'd birds sing, when indeed they cry.
>   (V, iv, 112)

Flamineo's sententious generalization about himself must be accepted on faith, for there has been no earlier demonstration of it. The thought is forgotten in the later scuffle. As it stands in the text, the most the soliloquy can tell about Flamineo's inner life is that his face, "full of smiles," is a mask, not wholly expressive of his sentiments.

In *The Duchess of Malfi* the soliloquy is used to no different end. Bosola, repenting of his treachery to the Duchess, would, within the frame of Shakespearian tragedy, conceivably be racked by an intense spiritual struggle, comparable to Enobarbus' suffering. Webster gives him two extended soliloquies on the subject of his treachery. Immediately after the Duchess' death he cries out:

> Oh sacred Innocence, that sweetly sleeps
> On Turtles' feathers: whil'st a guilty conscience
> Is a black Register, wherein is writ
> All our good deeds, and bad: a Perspective
> That shows us hell; that we cannot be suffer'd
> To do good when we have a mind to it!
> This is manly sorrow:
> These tears, I am very certain, never grew

In my Mother's Milk. My estate is sunk below
The degree of fear: where were these penitent fountains,
While she was living?
Oh, they were frozen up: here is a sight
As direful to my soul, as is the sword
Unto a wretch hath slain his father: Come,
I'll bear thee hence,
And execute thy last will; that's deliver
Thy body to the reverend dispose
Of some good women: that the cruel tyrant
Shall not deny me: Then I'll post to *Milan,*
Where somewhat I will speedily enact
Worth my dejection.

(IV, ii, 383)

Only the most tenuous interpretation could present this as a genuine explication of spiritual depth or as an insight into spiritual struggle. It states, rather, the results of a struggle which the audience is not permitted to see. It is thus the clarification of outer action: Bosola weeps and tells the audience of his guilty conscience. The audience is thereby informed how he feels about the death of the Duchess. Then he resolves on a new course of action. The soliloquy informs the audience that such a resolve has been formed, and prepares them for events to follow.

Similarly, in his soliloquy at the end of Act V, scene ii, Bosola meditates on the Cardinal's false sense of security and informs the audience that he will protect Antonio and perhaps join him in his revenge. Again this is a statement of resolve. Only at the end of the passage is there even the suggestion of something deeper:

Still methinks the Duchess
Haunts me: there, there! . . . 'tis nothing but my melancholy.
O Penitence, let me truly taste thy Cup,
That throws men down, only to raise them up.

(V, ii, 380)

But these words are all. Bosola, like Webster, veers away from the inward problem.

Just once does a Websterian soliloquy reveal the anguish of inner struggle. Toward the end of *The Duchess of Malfi,* the Cardinal enters with a book in hand, and says of the author he is reading,

> I am puzzl'd in a question about hell:
> He says, in hell, there's one material fire,
> And yet it shall not burn all men alike.
> Lay him by: How tedious is a guilty conscience!
> When I look into the Fish-ponds, in my Garden,
> Methinks I see a thing, arm'd with a Rake
> That seems to strike at me:
>
> (V, v, 1)

The emotional range and the evocative power of these lines are enormous. The Cardinal, thinking of hell, puts aside a question that might lead him to introspection, sighing the worldly cynicism that a guilty conscience is "tedious." Suddenly, his guilty meditations overcome him, and for the space of three lines, Webster bares the horrible psychological effects of his deeds on the man's inner being. The enigmatic image of the shapeless thing "arm'd with a Rake" beggars analysis. The power of the verse casts sudden light into the dark recesses of the Cardinal's soul, and for a moment the audience sees into the depths of his guilt. But it is a flash only—the spontaneous combustion of the image rather than a part of a systematically kindled general illumination.

In three of the four soliloquies quoted here, the word "conscience" is used as description and explanation of all mental and spiritual upset. This is implicit admission that the Websterian soliloquy does not attempt profound spiritual analysis. The recognition of a guilty conscience is the only acknowledgment of inner turmoil. It is cursory, undeveloped statement, revelatory of the effect of such turmoil rather than of the actual anguish.

The Character

The individuality of a character's behavior in the action of the play makes no greater revelation of his inner state of being than his soliloquies do. This is not to say that Webster's characters do not reveal themselves through their actions. They must and they do, but Webster tends to externalize as well as generalize these revelations by indicating how his chief figures conform in their behavior to a type—a type that is defined by the inclusion of formal descriptive passages in the manner of the *Characters* of Joseph Hall and Sir Thomas Overbury. As defined by Overbury, the Character is "a picture (real or personal) quaintly drawn in various colours, all of them heightened by one shadowing. It is a quick and soft touch of many strings, all shutting up in one musical close: it is wit's descant on any plain song."[5] A Character is essentially an epitomizing description, but it is the description of a type, not an individual personality, and is concerned with elements common to many, rather than with unique personal characteristics.

In 1615 forty-two Characters were added to the sixth edition of the Overbury collection. Thirty-two of these, marked with a separate title page, have been ascribed to Webster on the evidence of their similarity to passages in his plays.[6] If the attribution of these Characters is correct, Webster was probably writing them during the years of his great tragic period. Whether or not he actually wrote the specimens in the Overbury collection, it is clear that the medium was congenial to his thought and convenient to his purposes as a dramatist. Monticelso's "Character of a Whore" in *The White Devil* is an obvious example, and the opening scene of *The Duchess of Malfi* reveals that Webster conceived it necessary to present at the outset of his tragedy

formal Character descriptions of the leading personages. The
technique of description is exactly as prescribed by Overbury
for the writing of Characters. Antonio's description of the Cardinal is a full descant on the theme of the corrupt ecclesiast:

> he is a melancholy Churchman: The Spring in his face,
> is nothing but the Engendering of Toads: where he is
> jealous of any man, he lays worse plots for them, than
> ever was impos'd on *Hercules:* for he strews in his way
> Flatterers, Panders, Intelligencers, Atheists, and a
> thousand such political Monsters: he should have been
> Pope: but instead of coming to it by the primitive
> decency of the church, he did bestow bribes, so largely,
> and so impudently, as if he would have carried it away
> without heaven's knowledge.
>
> (*DM,* I, i, 158)

Thereafter, the Cardinal's behavior is consistent with this initial
"Characterization." A few lines later, he provides evidence for
the truth of Antonio's observations by ensuring that he will have
no nominal connection with the plan to install Bosola as a spy
in the Duchess' household. He says to Ferdinand:

> Be sure you entertain that *Bosola*
> For your Intelligence: I would not be seen in't.
> And therefore many times I have slighted him,
> When he did court our furtherance: as this Morning.
>
> (I, i, 235)

The subsequent action, indeed the major action after the death
of the Duchess, further reveals the treacherous hypocrisy of the
Cardinal as it is first presented.

To Webster, however, the Character was more than a technical convenience for character depiction. It was, in part at
least, a necessity to his tragic scheme. Character writing is a
product of eras when generalities and classifications are the tools
of psychological analysis. Aristotle and Theophrastus developed

the genre to describe cross sections of human nature. It retained
this generality when Hall and Overbury began their work with
it. Webster necessarily made the Characters in his tragedies
somewhat more individualized, as befitted the dramatic medium,
yet the generalizing element in the form remained, and it suited
his purpose well. By its use, he was able to provide his characters with a frame of reference that, while it did not deny them
on-stage reality, broadened their characteristics so that they became representatives of social types. The character traits of the
Cardinal in *The Duchess of Malfi* are those which, according to
popular supposition, would be possessed by any ambitious, unscrupulous Italian prelate. The Cardinal is explicitly viewed in
his relation to a recognizable type. His individuality is fitted into
a classification of society, and presented in terms of his external
behavior, and his later action, "heightened by one shadowing,"
becomes a generalized picture of the action of one kind of
human being. Like the other characters in Webster's tragic
scheme, he is to be made the subject for extensive satirical analysis, but the validity of that satire—on which so much of the
tragic effect depends—is determined by the degree to which the
Character makes the Cardinal seem a valid human specimen. To
satirize the villains of melodrama is to make mocks at scare-
crows. It is child's play, and in such action no truth is to be
found. To make a melodramatic villain true is quite another
matter, and certainly it cannot be accomplished without some
such generalizing technique as Webster used in the Character
descriptions.

Motivation

These uses of the soliloquy and the Character are indications of
a tendency on Webster's part to externalize and generalize the
people of the tragedies. His de-emphasis of their individuality
is further manifested in crucial actions where some of the char-

acters lose almost all personalizing traits. Particularly is this true
of those aligned with the forces of opposition: Francisco, Monticelso, Lodovico, and Gasparo in *The White Devil;* Ferdinand,
the Cardinal, and Bosola in *The Duchess of Malfi.* As the action
of each play progresses, it often appears that Vittoria and the
Duchess are oppressed not so much by individuals, feeling personal hatreds, desire for revenge, and lust to kill, as by representatives of destructive instincts in human nature, momentarily
abstracted from personal motivation. In very real ways, Webster keeps death, disease, insanity, and other forces which destroy men's bodies and souls before the minds of the audience.
In his presentation of character, he seems to imply that sometimes men become representative of such forces, losing almost
entirely the identification of individual motives in the wave of
destruction that carries them along. In *The White Devil,* for
example, Lodovico and Gasparo, dressed as Capuchins, their
identities hidden by monks' robes, enter the bedchamber of the
dying Brachiano and, under pretense of administering the sacra-
ment, whisper "some private meditations" to their victim.

> *Gasparo:*   *Brachiano!*
> *Lodovico:* Devil *Brachiano,*
>   Thou art damn'd.
> *Gasparo:*   Perpetually.
> *Lodovico:* A slave condemn'd, and given up to the gallows
>   Is thy great Lord and Master.
> *Gasparo:*   True: for thou
>   Art given up to the devil.
> *Lodovico:*   O you slave!
>   You that were held the famous Politician;
>   Whose art was poison.
> *Gasparo:*   And whose conscience murder.
> *Lodovico:* That would have broke your wife's neck down
>   the stairs
>   Ere she was poison'd.

Gasparo: That had your villainous sallets
Lodovico: And fine embroidered bottles,
   And perfumes
   Equally mortal with a winter plague.
Gasparo: Now there's Mercury—
Lodovico: And copperas—
Gasparo: And quick-silver—
Lodovico: With other devilish pothecary stuff
   A-melting in your politic brains: do'st hear?
Gasparo: This is Count *Lodovico*.
Lodovico: This, *Gasparo*.
   And thou shalt die like a poor rogue.
Gasparo: And stink
   Like a dead fly-blown dog.
Lodovico: And be forgotten before thy funeral sermon.
Brachiano: Vittoria! Vittoria!
             (V, iii, 149)

Although at the end they throw off their disguises and state their names, Lodovico and Gasparo seem for a moment devils incarnate rather than human beings. They are Bachiano's evils brought back to plague him. They pour whispered horror into his ears like poison—poison which the dying man himself has brewed. Their individual characteristics are blurred, fused into a single, momentarily anonymous force of destruction sweeping down on the person whose actions generated them into being.

Ferdinand, in *The Duchess of Malfi,* provides another example. His motives for torturing his sister are, to say the least, obscure. He gives them only after she is dead:

   . . . let me but examine well the cause;
   What was the meanness of her match to me?
   Only I must confess, I had a hope
   (Had she continu'd widow) to have gain'd
   An infinite mass of Treasure by her death:
   And that was the main cause; her Marriage—
   That drew a stream of gall quite through my heart.
             (IV, ii, 300)

Commentators have been at pains to point out that the "infinite mass of Treasure" could scarcely have been his, since there was a Duke of Malfi, the Duchess' son by her previous marriage. Faced with such weak motivation, some critics, responding to the implications of Ferdinand's more horrifying imagery, have suggested that Ferdinand had an incestuous love for his twin sister and tortures her because of his perverted jealousy. Whatever his motives, they are obscured by the madness that seizes him immediately after her death, and it is possible to hold that he acted as he did because of a congenital psychopathic condition which gave rise to his "most perverse, and turbulent Nature." This may explain Ferdinand, but it does not explain his partner in crime, the Cardinal, who has even less motivation and is far from insane.

The truth is that the great disparity between the causes of the Aragonian brothers' hatred and the punishment they exact cannot adequately be explained by any motivation in human terms. To gain Vittoria, Brachiano has his wife murdered. The murder has at least a motive, and it is accomplished without the elaborate embellishments of the Duchess' tortures. The death of the Duchess is more than a murder. It is an almost clinical investigation of the breaking point of the human spirit. Edmund Wilson, reviewing a wartime production of the tragedy in London, was reminded of the Nazi torture camps.[7] Like the horror there, the torture of the Duchess goes beyond normal human understanding. It is inconceivable that men should commit the crimes of Dachau; similarly there is no satisfactory human motivation for what Ferdinand does. Bosola to some extent shares this anonymity of motivation. He will not meet the Duchess in his own person, but assumes symbolical disguises: now a maker of tombs, now the common bellman who exhorts condemned criminals on the eve of execution. His individuality is partly lost in the storm of terror he comes to personify. In like manner, Ferdinand tends to lose his identity in the larger investigation. His action is abstracted from the personal level and becomes identified with the forces of destruction, the specters of rot, death, and social evil which fill the play.

Webster's tendency to identify individuals with the forces of oppression and mortality is further revealed by a technical device of his dialogue whereby a single point of view is shared by two men who speak antiphonally to attack a third person, as in the dialogue of Lodovico and Gasparo quoted above. The device occurs again in *The White Devil* in the arraignment scene and in the quarrel between Brachiano, Francisco, and Monticelso (II, i). In *The Duchess of Malfi,* Ferdinand and the Cardinal form a similar accusatory duet in their counsel against the Duchess' remarrying:

> *Cardinal:* We are to part from you: and your own discretion
>   Must now be your director.
> *Ferdinand:* You are a Widow:
>   You know already what man is: and therefore
>   Let not youth . . . high promotion, eloquence—
> *Cardinal:* No, nor any thing without the addition, *Honour,*
>   Sway your high blood.
> *Ferdinand:* Marry? they are most luxurious,
>   Will wed twice.
> *Cardinal:* O fie!
> *Ferdinand:* Their livers are more spotted
>   Than *Laban's* sheep.
>
> (I, i, 318)

They continue in this vein for fifty lines, until, as they leave, the Duchess says,

> I think this speech between you both was studied,
> It came so roundly off.
>
> (I, i, 367)

This curiously stylized dialogue served Webster as an instrument of great dramatic power. Here, as in *The White Devil,* he obtained the suggestion of a cumulative force of opposition to the individual, intense and relentless. Necessarily, the more sharply defined outlines of the characters blur as they merge with one another, but the abstract force of oppression comes clearer as a result. The effect is one of generalization, minimizing distinctions between members of the oppositional force, concentrating on outward action rather than inward character.

Webster, then, took a general view of man and his world and tried to depict the forces which played destructively upon individuality. His characters do not possess an inner reality. Only their outer nature is revealed, and even this is frequently absorbed into the panorama of general forces, with the result that the characters often lose even the exterior marks of their distinguishing individuality. After their chief traits have been described in the general terms of the formal Character, their subsequent behavior, seen in relation to the type to which they belong, suggests that their characteristics are shared by many others who could not be included on the stage. The soliloquy, which Shakespeare used to permit the audience deep insight into his characters, is used by Webster for expository purposes only. Indeed, in certain soliloquies he seems deliberately to turn his characters as well as his audience away from introspection and is content to depict the effect rather than the actuality of inner struggle. Finally, by removing the inner nature of man from his tragic picture, Webster indicates that he is not showing the development of his characters through suffering to an affirmation of moral good. Not development but stubborn consistency to self is the distinguishing element of Webster's tragic action.

It will be obvious to any reader of Shakespearian tragedy that these methods are unlike Shakespeare's. The difference is indicative of Webster's allegiance to Chapman. In their choice of tragic stories and in their ethical and political emphases, Webster and Chapman proceed in a similar manner to set their characters in action. Neither dramatist, however intense the scene, quite loses sight of the relation of the action to ethical precept. Neither finds place for significant representation of inner struggle and development of character, and both emphasize generality over individuality. Both make a virtue of stoic integrity and study this virtue in conflict with the disintegrating action of the Machiavels.

Yet at this point it becomes necessary to mark an essential difference. For Webster obviously does not follow Chapman all the way. Their basic philosophical positions are similar, but Chapman's stoicism was a much more positive, carefully formulated philosophy. His Machiavellism was, however, less dangerous, an altogether weaker force. Chapman could shape his tragic picture with more assurance. But Webster lacked such conviction, and without it he skirted the coasts of chaos. Yet, as a result of his sense of a less positive good and a stronger evil, he created characters of a subtlety and brilliance unknown to Chapman, and he imagined a world of shadows and doubt undreamt of in Chapman's philosophy.

CHAPTER THREE

THE TRAGIC CHARACTERS

Vittoria and Flamineo

VITTORIA COROMBONA is one of the fascinating characters in Jacobean drama. Devil she is, but woman too—a creature of immense capacity for evil and good together, an ingenious devil whose cleverness, come what may, is never at a loss, a woman who will fight courageously for what she holds most desirable. A "Devil in Crystal," Brachiano called her; "White Devil" was Webster's term for her. Lucas provides ample evidence that the phrase, in ordinary use, meant "hypocrite,"[1] and Charles Lamb's description, "innocence-resembling boldness," served to fasten this appellation on Vittoria. But such is the view of Vittoria from the judges' bench: in the minds of the judges, a known whore, yet one who refuses to admit her guilt, who comes before them with a proud, not a contrite heart. To be sure, Vittoria is no Magdalene. Hers is more nearly the way of the adulterous woman who "eateth and wipeth her mouth, and saith 'I have done no wickedness'."[2] But condemnation of Vittoria is not so simple as this. For Brachiano calls her a good woman; Flamineo finds her noble and loves her at the last. Goodness and nobility are two qualities which do not belong to the hypocrite. Nor does courage, nor fidelity, nor truth to oneself. Vittoria Corombona, despite her crimes, combines these qualities. In addition to "hypocrite," "White Devil" connotes here a woman who has in herself good and evil, courage and ruthlessness, truth and guilt, faith even as an adulteress.

In her first appearance, she reveals her capacity for violent feeling, her passion, and her courage. She has certain traits in common with her mother, if the violence of the scene with Cornelia in the first act is any indication. Cornelia has the same integrity, the willingness to face every situation at its worst, which Vittoria repeatedly manifests. In a lesser degree, Flamineo has this courage, and Marcello, from what is shown of him, seems to possess a similar integrity. But Vittoria and Flamineo are closest together. Both couple courage with ambition, becoming in the bargain completely ruthless. Flamineo will not hesitate to work for advancement by being Brachiano's pander, even at the cost of his own honor. Vittoria, partly for love, partly for the title of Duchess, will not stop at murder.

But here Flamineo and Vittoria part company. For Flamineo never manifests the capacity for feeling which Vittoria has and which partly sets her on her course of action. Both possess the family integrity, but with Flamineo this integrity is manifested in cynical disavowal of human feeling. As Lucas makes the contrast: "He embodies the cold clear intellect of the South as seen by Northern eyes, just as Vittoria on her side is the incarnation of its burning beauty and its haunting call. Machiavelli and Lucrezia Borgia—."[3] In Vittoria the avowal of a passionate nature is felt at once. To live by its dictates requires even more than for Flamineo to live by the dictates of his coldness, but brother and sister are allied in their integrity, and both live true to their inmost natures.

Shortly before she dies, Vittoria says, "I am too true a woman." It is this quality that, despite ambition and ruthlessness, makes her a brilliant figure. She is the incarnation of womanliness, *too* true a woman, for in herself she recognizes the immense wells of desire which cannot remain empty. Her husband is an impotent

pauper. Not a word of sympathy is wasted on him by either
faction. He is not the man to satisfy Vittoria's ambition or her
desire. When Brachiano comes along, she brushes Camillo aside.
This aspect of her nature is not presented as an excuse for her
conduct, but as a cause: Webster seems to feel that Vittoria's
behavior was as inevitable, under the circumstances, as it was
antisocial. When Cornelia breaks in upon the lovers in the
first act, she presents society's view of the liaison. She says to
Brachiano:

> The lives of Princes should like dials move,
> Whose regular example is so strong,
> They make the times by them go right or wrong. . . .
> Unfortunate *Camillo!*
>   (I, ii, 279, 282)

And to this, Vittoria replies:

> I do protest if any chaste denial,
> If any thing but blood could have allayed
> His long suit to me . . .
>   (I, ii, 283)

The word "blood" here denotes principally "passion." In the
same sense she puns on the word after she has been stabbed, and
her blood pours out over her hand:

> O my greatest sin lay in my blood.
> Now my blood pays for't.
>   (V, vi, 240)

Yielding to Brachiano is, to Vittoria, a necessity, for she cannot
deny the dictates of her passionate nature.[4]

Although Webster represents her sexual need for Brachiano
with considerable insight, this aspect of her character is not
developed, for to do more with it would perhaps have been
impossible so long as Vittoria was played by a boy. As it stands,
it is a daring stroke, equaled only by the relationship between

Beatrice Joanna and Deflores in *The Changeling*. But what follows is even more noteworthy: despite Vittoria's ruthlessness in
achieving her desires, once she has obtained them she remains
faithful. The only point at which she wavers in her love for
Brachiano is when he himself turns on her and calls her the
name she has suffered from the lips of all men. Even then her
wavering is only for a moment. She is true, always, to her nature,
convinced of the rightness, for herself, of her action.

Despite its ultimate virtue, such individualistic action cannot
be, for it cuts too broad a swath across the rights of society.
Vittoria's nature dooms her to act; her action dooms her to fail.
From this Webster did not draw the picture, as later dramatists
were to do, of a woman caught tragically in a conflict of heredity
and environment. He created, rather, a woman in whom good
and evil combine to baffle ordinary moral judgment. She cannot be tolerated by society, yet, because she is true to herself,
she cannot be entirely condemned. At least in the theater.

Perhaps the most interesting side of her character is revealed
in her relationship with her brother. Flamineo talks to her in the
role of Brachiano's servant. Yet he defends her honor against
Lodovico and appears willing to fight for her. His defense is
partly for his own honor, but he seems to feel some affection
for her. She has nothing for him but hatred, and turns him away
with only Cain's portion when he seeks a reward from her. She
attempts to trick him to death and, thinking him to be dying,
kicks him and treads upon his body. Having tried her faith to
him, Flamineo fully intends her death, and cries out to Lodovico
and Gasparo as they overpower him,

> You shall not take Justice from forth my hands,
> O let me kill her.—
>   (V, vi, 176)

But in the end, when he sees the way in which Vittoria meets
death, out of the flint of him is struck admiration.

> Th' art a noble sister,
> I love thee now; if woman do breed man,
> She ought to teach him manhood: Fare thee well.
>   (V, vi, 241)

Vittoria in her magnificence could command such love; she never gave it, never for a moment countenanced the man who in his way was nearest her in quality.

◇   ◇   ◇

The character of Flamineo is determined partly by his dramatic function as chorus for the author: he must be objective in the extreme. Yet this objectivity is an essential part of his character. He is passionless, cold and controlled except for flashes of anger. He dies as he lives, to himself.

> I do not look
> Who went before, nor who shall follow me;
> No, at my self I will begin and end.
>   (V, vi, 256)

Flamineo knows himself and has no illusions about his position, motives, or actions. His whole life is consumed with serving Brachiano so well as to merit and obtain preferment. Yet he is not one to flatter or to disguise his baseness. He acts within the limits which society sets upon him. His only legacy was the memory of his father's prodigality. Although he has a certain position in the world, he has no means of maintaining it. At the University of Padua he was little more than a menial, and this social hardship brought desire for power and wealth. A try at the life of a courtier taught him courtesy and lechery only. In his mature life, there is nothing for him unless he succeeds in Brachiano's services. The bitterness of his position has brought disillusion and cynicism.

It is strange that this man, so lacking in sympathy, can in any

measure arouse the sympathy of the audience. Yet there is
attractiveness in his mercurial disposition, his gay yardage of
words, his frank embracement of the loathsome. His most compelling claim to sympathy is that he, like Vittoria, possesses a
kind of integrity. He has his standards, however abhorrent they
may seem, and lives by them. He is what he is, an agent for
himself, in the face of all opposition, all ties of loyalty, indeed
of all the good in human life. Milton's Satan under somewhat
similar conditions becomes heroic. Flamineo becomes at least
sympathetic.

This can be seen more clearly by contrasting him with Brachiano, who, despite his greatness, lacks this self-integrity. There
is no word of excuse or justification for Brachiano. He is the
man of passion and power, the epitome of the Italian duke. To
be sure, he acts with the reckless courage of a great man. He
is ready to make war to defend his actions; he does things in the
grand manner. But underneath this splendor there is meanness.
As Lucas says, "He has neither goodness nor real greatness."[5]
He was, however, the man Vittoria loved, and though he failed
her and doubted her, yet he loved her. Dying, he calls for her:

> Where's this good woman? had I infinite worlds
> They were too little for thee. Must I leave thee?
>
> (V, iii, 18)

His last words as he is strangled are her name, repeated in a
desperate, terrible cry. This stirs sympathy for him, and perhaps
colors the final evaluation of his character. Nevertheless, an
audience, though it might forgive, would be unlikely to forget
that passion moves him in ways that it never moves Vittoria. His
wavering comes perilously close to destroying his love for her.
Policy, too, turns him from his chosen course. He makes a
patched peace with Francisco and Monticelso as they threaten
war. At one moment he thinks affectionately of his son. At the

next, he turns on his wife brutally, in the cruelest scene in either tragedy. Desire once felt and action determined, like Vittoria he stops at nothing; but the murder of Isabella is by no means to be brushed aside so lightly as the death of Camillo. Webster makes this felt even in the manner of her death, from poison placed on the lips of her husband's picture which it was her nightly habit to kiss. Brachiano's dissembling of sorrow at the news of her death is disgusting. Far better is Vittoria's unsympathetic reception of the news of Camillo's murder. Far better is Flamineo's dispassionate objectivity. These attitudes have at least their openness to recommend them. Brachiano seems little more than a magnificent hypocrite.

The Duchess and Bosola

The Duchess of Malfi, superficial differences aside, has much in common with Vittoria Corombona. Although she might appear to be a development of Isabella rather than a sister-under-the-skin to Vittoria, it is truer to say that the Duchess is Vittoria, evil purged, passionate temperament alchemized to gentleness and sympathy. The Duchess would not have been capable of making the sacrifice which Isabella makes for Brachiano. To her, such sacrifice would involve loss of dignity and honor, for she is much more the noblewoman than Brachiano's wife. In this, she is closer to Vittoria. Both women maintain their individuality and their integrity above all things. Both, in different ways, possess courage and faith; neither will swerve from a chosen course, once it is deemed right. But here the resemblance ends, and the Duchess emerges as a woman in her own right.

One of Webster's little-noted accomplishments is his skilled reproduction of the social atmosphere of a small Italian duchy. A group of people, compact about the ruler, and controlled by his whims and desires—Amalfi is a duchy of this sort, and its

ruler is a woman secure in her social position. The play opens
on a scene of social life in this court. The visitors, Ferdinand
and his courtiers, reproduce the small talk of a prince and his
followers. There is discussion of "chargeable Revels" and the
large expense of "these Triumphs" with which the Duchess has
entertained her brothers. Evidently, she is a woman to whom
the social world is important, who (a comparison might be made
with the Countess of Pembroke or with Elisabetta Gonzaga)
built a world around her which she understood and into which
she fitted perfectly. Webster possibly had a deliberate reason
for giving her no name but her title. She is always, in all things,
the Duchess of Malfi. On her world and her position, her life
is grounded. Her reputation, as she says, is more than life.

Antonio's Character of her need not be quoted. He is a man
in love and speaks with privileged bias of his lady. Yet she lives
true to his picture in every way, the gentle and gracious lady.
But underneath this graciousness is firmness. She has something
of her brothers in her, as Vittoria and Flamineo share family
traits. Controlled by goodness and breeding, the Duchess is,
nevertheless, as much an individual in her willfulness as Ferdinand or the Cardinal, and shows herself at the outset a woman
not easily swayed by others. Her brothers dictatorially forbid her
to remarry. Ferdinand wishes her to remain single the rest of
her life; the Cardinal, perhaps, would countenance a marriage
with "the addition, *Honour*." Upon hearing their grim warnings,
the Duchess keeps her self-possession and even jokes at their
seriousness. When the Cardinal leaves, Ferdinand threatens her
and speaks disgustingly to her. She rebukes him and, immediately afterward, when he too has gone, says,

> Shall this move me? if all my royal kindred
> Lay in my way unto this marriage:
> I'd make them my low foot-steps . . .
> So I, through frights, and threatenings, will assay

This dangerous venture: Let old wives report
I winked, and chose a husband: *Cariola,*
To thy known secrecy, I have given up
More than my life, my fame.

(I, i, 382, 392)

This immediate decision, in spite of ominous threats, shows the power of will of a Vittoria. But there is a difference. Rather than fight where an open breach would bring disaster, the Duchess avoids conflict, still proceeding on her own way. The difference is the difference in the social position of the two women.

As soon as the Duchess determines her course of action, she summons Antonio, and there follows the extraordinarily beautiful proposal scene. It is Webster's loveliest music, a harmony he struck too seldom and which even now is jarred by the first dissonances of the hideous cacophony to come. For the moment, the music rises sweetly to its culmination in the lyric duet of the pledging of marriage vows. The lovers go out. Cariola remains behind and says,

Whether the spirit of greatness, or of woman
Reign most in her, I know not, but it shows
A fearful madness. I owe her much of pity.

(I, i, 576)

The spirit of greatness or the spirit of woman: the spirit of implacable defiance of the worst of fate or the spirit of submission; the spirit of courage or the spirit of fear; of integrity or death. These are the forces which are brought into sharp conflict within Webster's heroine. It is the spirit of woman which will threaten to destroy her integrity. Through her womanish fears, evil will cause her to betray her greatness and bring her, possessed of a "fearful madness," to the verge of the destructive escape insanity provides. Significantly, the first act ends with the words "pity" and "fear." Cariola sounds the portents of tragedy.

When next the Duchess appears, the "fearful madness" is

materializing. Here, as he explores the effects of pregnancy on his heroine, Webster introduces her tendency toward hysteria—in this scene, an unsettled whimsicality made manifest in her irritability and moody trifling with court ceremony — which nearly destroys her in the end. This is the spirit of woman, which, when it mounts higher in her than the spirit of greatness, endangers the world and the reputation on which she depends. Not that she is unable to fight for what she possesses. At the test, her love for Antonio is greater than her love for her world, but even love must not be allowed to cause her to forget her essential majesty. If ever she is false to herself she will be destroyed. Her behavior when flight becomes necessary, when she is banished from the shrine at Loreto, and when she is forced to part from Antonio, is in every way dignified. But dignity is achieved only by courageous struggle. She does not fight as Vittoria does, in an open brawl. The Duchess must put down the spirit of woman and behave as the spirit of greatness dictates. To do this requires fully as much courage as Vittoria possessed.

In the fourth act the balance of the spirit of woman and the spirit of greatness is nearly upset. The Duchess can fight oppression, can surmount obstacles, such as the flight to Ancona, but the test comes as she is pulled lower and lower by the violence that touches her own person, body and mind. Bosola describes her as she appears when she is first imprisoned:

> She's sad, as one long us'd to't: and she seems
> Rather to welcome the end of misery
> Than shun it: a behavior so noble,
> As gives a majesty to adversity:
> You may discern the shape of loveliness
> More perfect, in her tears, than in her smiles;
> She will muse four hours together: and her silence,
> (Methinks) expresseth more, than if she spake.

(IV, i, 4)

Thus far, as Bosola admits with admiration, she has been the great lady and has preserved her integrity. Now Webster casts a concentrate of evil upon her and tortures her beyond understanding, surrounds her last moments with all the horrors of hell. The purpose is to see if a force of pure, motiveless evil can shake her fundamental integrity. Everything for which the Duchess stood is destroyed in this act. Her world is reduced to her prison, her husband and eldest son apparently murdered, her reputation slandered, her sanity endangered.

More important than the conflict between the Duchess and her brothers in this act is the relation between the Duchess and Bosola. The brothers in their inflictions have passed human comprehension. Their acts of oppression are symbolic of destructive forces beyond motivation. But Bosola is no fiend. At the outset of the play he manifests great distaste for his work. In the Cardinal's service he has fallen into the galleys. He returns, desperate for a living. The other people in the play find a goodness in him that was never known in Flamineo. Antonio says,

> 'Tis great pity
> He should be thus neglected—I have heard
> He's very valiant: This foul melancholy
> Will poison all his goodness.
> (I, i, 75)

His desperation, like Flamineo's, makes him resolve upon a life of criminal service, and once the resolution is made, he cleaves to it. He is absolutely loyal to his master, numbing himself to the condition of an automaton when he is forced to the cruelties of the fourth act. Yet he bears no love for his master. Ferdinand, he thinks, grossly flatters himself; and, as the play progresses, many small frictions develop between them.

Ferdinand, in his turn, underestimates his man's strength of character. He sets no store by Bosola's scruples at acting as a spy. "Be your self," he says, and Bosola replies with bitter self-awareness, "I am your creature." Bosola's difficulty is that he knows he is *not* himself. He sells out. By his intelligencing, as he says, he "forfeits his own shape." Fundamentally a man of character, he has become the creature of a man he despises. For temporal reasons of expediency, he gives over being true to what he essentially is. But he is not Flamineo. Bosola—this is the shock at the heart of his villainy—is a moral man. Flamineo has seen the world as venal and adjusted to it. Bosola sees it as mortal; but, short of death, no peace is possible. He therefore compromises with his moral sense, but at the same time falls into the habit of self-criticism, publicly exposing his depravity as a kind of indecent apology for his lack of integrity. His awareness of self causes him to be sharply critical of others, and he becomes an ironist in all he says and does. Thus far, the pattern of life his character sets for him is not unlike Flamineo's. But for Bosola, ironical neutrality is untenable. He feels too strongly about life, and needs the sense of value which truth to his essential nature alone would provide.

Bosola has none of Flamineo's native coldness. His is an attitude of forced dispassion. Although he must persecute the Duchess, he feels increasing sympathy for her. He watches her carefully and seems aware that she is holding in precarious balance the spirit of greatness and the spirit of woman. It is not necessary, from his point of view, to save her life. Human life is insignificant. The only possible value is the preservation of one's essential nature in the face of adversity. It is vitally necessary to Bosola that the Duchess shall not prove false to herself by giving way to "womanish fears." He admires her, and in the act of, even by means of, persecution, struggles to preserve in her the very integrity he has betrayed in himself. His position, therefore, is the epitome of irony: betraying himself by his loyalty to Ferdinand, being true to himself in his betrayal of the Duchess.

In Bosola, the balance between truth and falsity is upset. Falsity gains the dominance, and Bosola, for a time, is unable to right the scales.

Bosola's function of arousing the spirit of greatness in the Duchess is apparent in the first catastrophe. The Duchess makes hasty plans for flight, proposing to follow Antonio north to Ancona as soon as possible. Bosola counsels her differently:

> I would wish your Grace, to feign a Pilgrimage
> To our Lady of *Loreto,* (scarce seven leagues
> From fair *Ancona*)—so may you depart
> Your Country, with more honour, and your flight
> Will seem a Princely progress, retaining
> Your usual train about you.
>
> (III, ii, 353)

He can have no ulterior reason for giving this counsel, and there is nothing to prevent the audience from taking it at face value. Bosola's thought here seems to be that what has to come will come, and consequently it is better for the Duchess to meet adversity with dignity than to behave like a frightened girl.

When Antonio is forced to escape from Amalfi, the Duchess, partly to conceal Antonio's real reason for flight and partly to test Bosola's loyalty, says that Antonio was "basely descended." Bosola replies with an oblique praise of Antonio that is apparently sincere:

> Will you make your self a mercenary herald,
> Rather to examine men's pedigrees, than virtues?
>
> (III, ii, 300)

Yet, when he captures the Duchess at Ancona, he refers to Antonio as a "base, low-fellow. . . . One of no Birth." This double opinion which Bosola appears to hold of Antonio would seem to be either inconsistent or hypocritical. Actually it is neither. Bosola, in the second instance, is rousing the spirit of greatness in the Duchess at the moment when her hysterical behavior threatens to give the spirit of woman the upper hand. The means he uses are important to an understanding of the fourth act.

The Duchess, separated from Antonio and facing imprisonment, reveals her state of mind by crying distractedly that she will fly in pieces "like to a rusty o'er-charg'd Cannon." Her children cannot yet talk,

> But I intend, since they were born accurs'd;
> Curses shall be their first language.
>
> (III, v, 137)

This excessive, undignified language is reminiscent of that in the scene in which Bosola shatters her composure with jests about the apricots. Bosola, sensing the danger in her mounting emotionality, offers her pity and safety, but this produces only hysteria. Then, with anger stirring in him, he urges, almost commands, her to forget her lowborn, beggarly husband. Instantly she takes hold of herself. "Say that he was born mean," she cries,

> Man is most happy, when's own actions
> Be arguments, and examples of his Virtue.
>
> (III, v, 144)

She tells him the moral fable of the salmon and the dogfish, and, in a calmer state of mind, goes to her imprisonment "arm'd 'gainst misery." Thus, by deliberately debasing someone close to the Duchess' heart, Bosola has forced her to assert her majesty in defense of what she holds dear. She forgets the womanish fears for her own safety, and Bosola, for the moment, has succeeded in protecting her from herself.

So, in the dark fourth act, Bosola carries on his double role of executioner and bellman. It was the bellman's function to exhort the condemned man to pray God for forgiveness and

thus enable him to meet death with fortitude. This is the last
service Bosola renders to the Duchess. As the moments of physical horror grow more intense and more frequent, the Duchess
sometimes threatens to give way to womanish sorrow unbefitting
a noblewoman. At first she bears her imprisonment well and
retains a "majesty in adversity," as Bosola says. Then Ferdinand
comes to her in the darkened room. She waits in silence for him
to speak and, because he has signified his wish to make peace
with her, asks his pardon. He goes, leaving behind him the dead
man's hand. Suddenly, to add to the Duchess' bewilderment, the
traverse is drawn, revealing the bodies of her husband and son.
Of this sight Bosola says characteristic words that show the way
his mind turns toward arming the Duchess against misery:

> He doth present you this sad spectacle,
> That now you know directly they are dead,
> Hereafter you may (wisely) cease to grieve
> For that which cannot be recovered.
>   (IV, i, 68)

But his philosophy only makes the Duchess increasingly hysterical. The spirit of woman rises high in her, and her mind runs
to exaggerated and distracted images: it would be a mercy

> If they would bind me to that lifeless trunk,
> And let me freeze to death.
>   (IV, i, 79)

Bosola tries to counsel her: despair is not fitting, "remember/
You are a Christian." At first his efforts are to dissuade her
from her grief as best he can. He tells her to seek refuge in
her faith, then that he pities her and will save her life. But, thinking Antonio dead, she will not take comfort. Bosola's pity brings
out her womanish fears, and, her controls almost gone, she turns
wildly to curse the stars.

For a moment the Duchess is truly mad. The rational connec-

tives of language disappear. She is "full of daggers," and thinks
herself covered with vipers. Suddenly she sees a servant in the
room. "What are you?" she asks. The servant replies quietly,
"One that wishes you long life." The unexpected significance
of the reply penetrates her madness; she seizes its meaning
tenaciously.

> I would thou wert hang'd for the horrible curse
> Thou hast given me: I shall shortly grow one
> Of the miracles of pity: I'll go pray: No,
> I'll go curse.
>
> (IV, i, 110)

There follows a chain of protective thought, a passionate intel-
lectuality that focuses on the words with such intensity as to
suggest that words alone can save her.

> *Duchess:*   I'll go pray: No,
>   I'll go curse:
> *Bosola:* Oh fie!
> *Duchess:* I could curse the Stars.
> *Bosola:* Oh fearful!
> *Duchess:* And those three smiling seasons of the year
>   Into a Russian winter: nay the world
>   To its first Chaos.
> *Bosola:* Look you, the Stars shine still:
> *Duchess:* Oh, but you must remember, my curse hath a
>   great way to go:
>   Plagues, (that make lanes through largest families)
>   Consume them! . . .
>
> (IV, i, 112)

And she proceeds with her curse against the stars. With reason
almost gone, it seems as if her mind takes refuge in the image,
developing it in terms of time and space, with an almost logical
explanation of the fact that her curse has no immediate effect.
To keep from breaking entirely, she seems subconsciously to be

forcing herself to concentrate on an idea, any idea, as a last safeguard against insanity. In relation to her present situation, this dwelling on words is meaningless, but for the Duchess there is no other way. She must cling to the rational thread of the image to save herself. Otherwise, it is clear, the way she is going is truly the way madness lies.

Bosola's responses to her words are important. As she breaks under his sympathy, he shifts his ground and suddenly turns to mockery: "Oh fie!" "Oh fearful!" He marks, by his attitude toward her hysteria, the impotence of the Duchess in the presence of disintegrating evil. Her sense of her own importance, implicit in her curse against the traditional symbols of Fate, the stars, is turned against her. For all her imprecations, Bosola tells her, she can have no external control over her destiny. Bosola's move now is to shatter her illusions, to bring her face to face with what he feels to be the essential realities of the situation. He will not let her escape: insanity is too easy. She must conquer by staring down the powers that seek to destroy her. And if philosophy and charity will not cause her to see through to the truth about human life, then satire, the ultimate weapon for stripping illusion, must do it. "Look you, the Stars shine still." Webster wrote no more disillusioning line than this.

Bosola is motivated by more than Ferdinand's order. The persecution of the Duchess goes beyond his farthest expectations. "Why do you do this?" he asks the Duke at the end of the first scene. "To bring her to despair." Bosola replies,

> 'Faith, end here:
> And go no farther in your cruelty—
> Send her a penitential garment, to put on,
> Next to her delicate skin, and furnish her
> With beads, and prayer books.
>   (IV, i, 141)

But Ferdinand will not hear this. He lashes himself to the point where he conceives of setting the madmen loose on her. This is more than Bosola can bear.

> *Bosola:* Must I see her again?
> *Ferdinand:* Yes.   *Bosola:* Never.
> *Ferdinand:* You must.
> *Bosola:* Never in mine own shape,
>   That's forfeited, by my intelligence,
>   And this last cruel lie: when you send me next,
>   The business shall be comfort.
>   (IV, i, 158)

Ferdinand, not understanding him, replies,

> Very likely!—
> Thy pity is nothing of kin to thee.
>   (IV, i, 165)

But the comfort Bosola intends is not pity.

When the Duchess next appears, the madness is close upon her. As she says,

>   nothing but noise, and folly
> Can keep me in my right wits, whereas reason
> And silence, make me stark mad.
>   (IV, ii, 6)

She sits in numb silence, sleeping "like a mad-man" with her eyes open. And yet,

>   I'll tell thee a miracle—
> I am not mad yet, to my cause of sorrow.
> Th' heaven o'er my head, seems made of molten brass,
> The earth of flaming sulphur, yet I am not mad;
> I am acquainted with sad misery,
> As the tann'd galley-slave is with his Oar,
> Necessity makes me suffer constantly,
> And custom makes it easy—
>   (IV, ii, 25)

There is no surface indication here of the charming woman she

once was. Everything she has had and everything she has stood
for have been taken from her. To Cariola she is like a ruined
monument. To herself she is little more than a slave. The madmen enter, the Duchess' last audience, and after them Bosola,
who, unable to face her, has renounced his own shape and disguised himself. He tells her he has come to make her tomb.
Despite her earlier despair this sudden reference to her tomb
startles her.

> Hah, my tomb?
> Thou speak'st, as if I lay upon my death bed,
> Gasping for breath: do'st thou perceive me sick?
> ### (IV, ii, 116)

Bosola's answer shows that he is fully cognizant of the source of
her misery:

> Yes, and the more dangerously, since thy sickness is
>   insensible.
> ### (IV, ii, 119)

Bosola knows this much: Ferdinand is not to be placated. He
himself cannot or will not help her to escape. All that can be
done for her is to cause her to reassert her majesty. This he had
accomplished once before, on the Ancona road, quieting her hysteria by attacking her husband's reputation. In the same way he
now rids her of the "insensible sickness" by pulling from her all
"vanities," analyzing even her body in its lowest elemental
terms. The earth, the men and women on it, he tells her, are
nothing. Social distinction is of no importance when death has
become a law of life. She is merely a woman whose worldly
position has accentuated her suffering and her mortality.

> Thou art a box of worm-seed, at best, but a salvatory
> of green mummy: what's this flesh? a little crudded
> milk, fantastical puff-paste: our bodies are weaker than
> those paper prisons boys use to keep flies in: more con-

temptible: since ours is to preserve earth-worms: didst thou ever see a Lark in a cage? such is the soul in the body: this world is like her little turf of grass, and the Heaven o'er our heads, like her looking glass, only gives us a miserable knowledge of the small compass of our prison. . . . Thou are some great woman sure, for riot begins to sit on thy forehead (clad in gray hairs) twenty years sooner, than on a merry milk-maid's. Thou sleep'st worse, than if a mouse should be forc'd to take up her lodging in a cat's ear: a little infant, that breeds its teeth, should it lie with thee, would cry out, as if thou wert the more unquiet bed-fellow.

                    (IV, ii, 123, 138)

This last, strangely tender abasement of her rouses her from her insensible sickness.[6] The fearful madness is put behind. Bosola's speech is punctuated by a crescendo of assertion:

Who am I? . . .
Am not I, thy Duchess? . . .
I am Duchess of *Malfi* still.

The final assertion of her greatness disperses the storm of terror which Ferdinand has summoned. Death, stripped bare of horror, is welcome, and she hears the dirge with composure, makes arrangements for her children, and turns to her executioners. "Now what you please, / What death?"

Bosola's intention has been to make her see herself and her situation as they essentially are, and to hold to her greatness in defiance of mortality. At this moment he faces her with the last test. He suddenly produces the strangling cord and holds it before her eyes. "The manner of your death should much afflict you," he says. "This cord should terrify you?" His curiosity contains his last hope, frightening in its intensity.[7] The Duchess answers calmly, "Not a whit." Yet, as she looks at the cord, she seems to draw in upon herself, stifling emotion, lapsing into the repressed hysteria of the insensible sickness. She speaks numbly:

> Not a whit—
> What would it pleasure me, to have my throat cut
> With diamonds? or to be smothered
> With Cassia? or to be shot to death, with pearls?
> I know death hath ten thousand several doors
> For men, to take their *Exits:* and 'tis found
> They go on such strange geometrical hinges,
> You may open them both ways: . . .
> (IV, ii, 221)

The sudden swell of fantastic imagery in contrast to the ugly reality of the strangling cord makes clear that, as in the cursing of the stars, the Duchess is escaping reality in an elaborate, over-wrought image. Physically she does not flinch. But her mind, almost in reflex action, draws away from death in a moment of unexpressed terror. But this time she does not need Bosola's help to triumph. Instead, she manages deliberate renunciation of the fantastic imagery, brushing it and her terror aside in a word:

> They go on such strange geometrical hinges,
> You may open them both ways: any way, (for heaven sake)
> So I were out of your whispering.
> (IV, ii, 227)

The verbal concatenation ("ways . . . way") marks the moment of release. A sudden rush of emotion breaks through the protective shell of death images which have masked her terror, and the insensible sickness is dispelled. Now she is free from the danger of insanity, able to make her peace with herself before the "immense night" closes in. At the end she faces death untroubled by the horror which surrounds it.

> Tell my brothers,
> That I perceive death, (now I am well awake)
> Best gift is, they can give, or I can take—
> (IV, ii, 229)

The words "now I am well awake" mark the end of the sickness. Stunned and almost broken with horror, she has been forced to the brink of madness in order to escape the contemplation of death. Only at the last can she disperse the mist of terror which has prevented her dignified acceptance of her fate. The spirit of greatness mounts high in her, and as for the spirit of woman:

> I would fain put off my last woman's-fault,
> I'd not be tedious to you.
>
> (IV, ii, 232)

The woman's fault is left for Cariola. The Duchess, firm in her resolve, and fixing her faith in heaven, goes quietly to her death.

What remains to be said can be briefly told. The remorse and madness in Ferdinand and the tedious guilty conscience of the Cardinal parallel Bosola's assertion of pity and shame when he takes it upon himself to be her avenger. The last act shows forces of horror spending themselves in destruction, beyond human control. Then all collapses, and what is left is the memory of the Duchess' greatness. Pity for her is eased by admiration; tears have come from a deeper source than those that were shed for Isabella. For the Duchess as for Vittoria, superficial emotion is deepened by the recognition that whatever has happened, whether just or unjust, these women in their suffering have preserved their integrity.

These are the important individuals in the two tragedies, and it is possible now to clarify the generalizations with which earlier chapters have been concerned. That these characters do not reveal significant spiritual growth is apparent. They struggle against mighty opposition to maintain their integrity. What may appear to be development in Bosola, from a thing of evil to a man filled with remorse, is in fact no more than a return to what he essentially is. He is the example of a man who has lost integrity of life. He has put aside his essential nature, forfeiting

his "own shape" in order to serve Ferdinand, and in so doing
has been false to himself. Only in the end, when the Duchess is
dead, does his integrity reassert itself. But it is then too late for
redemption.

He fares no worse than the other characters, for in Webster's
world there is no justice, no law, either of God or man, to mete
out punishment for evil and reward for good. Death itself is not
justice but the normal course of events, the culmination of spiritual and physical decay. Honor and revenge do not signify in
the end, for, whether the death be violent or natural, it is always
a working out through men of forces larger than man. Evil and
good are dragged down together in death, just as they are meshed
together in life. The only triumph comes when, even in the
moment of defeat, an individual is roused to assert his own integrity of life. This is not a question of virtue and vice. In Webster's tragic world, characters are significant not because of their
morality but because of their struggle. Some lose their identities
in the forces of evil. Some die in the attempt to preserve the
good. But ultimately it is the struggling ones, the splendid fight-
ers for self, who matter.

It is as if the world were an immense jungle, steaming and
rotten with disease, haunted by the sudden unseen treacheries
of man. Here and there a magnificent individual rises, fighting
to hack his way free of the matted tendrils. As surely as his
individuality asserts itself in positive action, hands stretch forth
to pull him back into the darkness. Men and women in this
world are linked by one inescapable bond: they are involved in
common mortality. Man's evil and the world's decay only con-
strict the cords of involvement which tighten slowly about the
throat. "Strangling is a very quiet death," and they are few who,
fighting it, can cry once sharply of the essential glory in man.

To speak metaphorically of the characters in Webster's tragic
world is sometimes the best way of accomplishing the critical

end. In the large view, the characters appear to lose their minute distinctions. One is aware of forces at work, of struggle going on, but it is the general picture that matters most. As detail melts into the whole, it is the tragic world, not the tragic protagonist, which becomes the significant aspect of Webster's work. All else blurs into the large panorama. F. L. Lucas writes:

> Of Webster's characters in general, . . . we may say that they are painted with a broad brush that does not exclude, now and then, a sudden delicacy of touch. They fill an adequate place on his canvas, though they seldom step out of the frame into the world, to continue existing with all the reality of living people we have known, as does a Falstaff or a Hamlet. . . . However let us grant that it is not so much for his characters that Webster is remembered, as for the light and darkness he was able to cast across them as they moved, his power to make them the mouthpieces of the poetry both of great instants and of eternity, the embodiments of a dying dream.[8]

To attempt to put the matter more concretely than this is perhaps hazardous, for, at any given moment on the stage, the characters have all the life and reality which a drama requires. Yet their individuality diminishes when viewed against the panoramic background Webster painted. They have the qualities of good and evil which men and women have in life. But oppression and struggle mount beyond what they are in life, and consequently are lifted out of the normal atmosphere. Behind the figures on the stage lie forces of which they are agents, and it is these forces, unseen in the world of ordinary reality, that impress the audience as being of general concern. *The White Devil* and *The Duchess of Malfi* together depict a world that is horrifying. But it is the world, rather than any individual in it, which apparently interested Webster most vitally. Any discussion of Websterian tragedy must, therefore, concern itself with the full panorama of Webster's tragic vision of life, and with the satiric techniques which he used to express that vision.

PART TWO

The Satiric Design

CHAPTER FOUR # W EBSTER

and MARSTON

CHAPMAN'S ETHICAL VISION was steady, his approach to the problem of the good, positive. With his pattern of the complete man before him, he measured and judged the ethical stature of individuals in his world with ease. For him, evil, as well as good, was obvious and relatively uncomplicated.

Other playwrights with less readiness of conviction, however, found that evil was not so easily understood or characterized. It appeared unexpectedly in the fairest show; it corrupted, like disease, from within; and it ensnared the unsuspecting from without. To many of the dramatists—Tourneur is a notable instance—the world seemed so warped with viciousness that no positive measure of conduct was to be found. The corruption represented by the popular Machiavellian villain made Castiglione's courtier a wistful fiction. Chapman's complete man wandered alone in a wasteland, and at best was an examplar of a moralist's theory of what should be, rather than of what is. For these dramatists, to whom the problems of evil were more pressing than ideas about good, dramatists who, presumably, could not be content with Fletcherian fantasies, there was little recourse but to look on evil as steadily as possible, to expose it, and to hope that some positive consequence would result from bringing a "nest of snakes" to light. There was, in short, little recourse for them but satire.

To an Elizabethan, satire meant the stripping of illusion, the facing of the stark ugliness of the world, and the flaying of abuses. Their formal verse satires were blunt, open rebukes of vice, making little use of such scalpel ironies as Dryden and Swift were later to develop in English. The model, both in form and in tone, was, of course, Latin satire. O. J. Campbell notes that "the inchoate roughness of Lucilius, the severity of Juvenal's invective, and the bitterness and obscurity of Persius confirmed the Renaissance satirists in their determination to be downright and raw."[1]

John Marston, who had made a reputation as a verse satirist, before he turned to the drama in 1599, provides several partial definitions of his own satiric aims and methods. In the Epilogue to *Pygmalion's Image,* he suggests the prevailing tone:

> I'll snarl at those which do the world beguile
> With maskëd shows.

Again, in the *Proemium* to the third book of *The Scourge of Villainy,* he states his aim:

> In serious jest, and jesting seriousness,
> I strive to scourge polluting beastliness;
> I invoke no Delian deity, . . .
> But grim Reproof, stern Hate of villainy. . . .
> Fair Detestation of foul odious sin,
> In which our swinish times like wallowing,
> Be thou my conduct and my genius,
> My wits-inciting, sweet-breath'd Zephyrus.
> Oh that a Satire's hand had force to pluck
> Some floodgate up, to purge the world from muck!
>   (1, 18)

The directness and the rawness are evident even in such relatively temperate passages as these, and Marston's techniques are not substantially different from those of his contemporaries.

During the last decade of the sixteenth century, Hall, Breton, Donne, Marston, and others chorused their snarls at courtier and whore, churchman and fool, politician and pander. Their intention was to reform the vicious and warn the errant through the realistic depiction of evil and folly. Yet the intention was obviously more pious than practical. Their rage at best was frustrate. Like Marlowe's personification of Wrath, it turned on itself when it "had nobody to fight withal," and London was briefly presented with the spectacle of satirist scourging satirist. Eventually, this reformatory zeal was swallowed by a gross, even pathological, investigation of vice, instructive and delightful only to the vicious. The satirist was engulfed by the muck he sought to purge.[2]

For the particular offense that satire had become, the purge was fire, not flood. In 1599, on the authority of the Archbishop of Canterbury and the Bishop of London, the satires were publicly burned, and their further publication forbidden. The year is significant. Almost at once, Ben Jonson adapted some of the satiric techniques to the uses of his "comical satire" plays, and, in the noncomic drama, the satiric plays of John Marston appeared.

Marston, here, is the key figure. Practicing both tragedy and satire, he provides firm evidence for the link between the two. Chiefly because of Marston's influence, much of the serious drama after the turn of the century was informed by the spirit, the subject matter, and the techniques of Elizabethan verse satire. His early tragedies, *Antonio and Mellida* and *Antonio's Revenge,* are noteworthy experiments in adapting the techniques of his satire to the tragic stage, and it is important to the present concern to see that Webster knew his Marston as well as his Chapman. Webster and Marston are linked by an oblique collaboration, since Webster wrote the *Induction* to Marston's most

successful satiric play, *The Malcontent*. Even without this connection, there is plentiful though less specific evidence from the
plays to show that Webster derived suggestions from Marston's
tragic style. Marston, indeed, is second only to Chapman as a
formative influence on *The White Devil* and *The Duchess of
Malfi*.[3]

The Revenge of Virtue on Vice

Marston's satire is anything but pleasant. Its verse is harsh,
jangling, crabbed; its subject matter, as it should be, is disaf-
fecting; and frequently its moral attitude is little better than one
of the wicked. Yet, in the midst of his spying out of enormities,
Marston maintains at least the notion of satiric purgation. The
satiric element of his early tragedy is not significantly different,
for at first he merely dramatized his traditional subject matter
and converted many of his satiric techniques to stage purposes.

The first part of *Antonio and Mellida,* a comedy only by virtue
of its happy ending, is Marston's earliest attempt at dramatic
satire. Here he isolates his satiric material from the main story
by confining it to a plotless series of scenes in which the self-
sufficient, objective Felice comments on the fools and court
flatterers about him. Felice describes his role in the play as
"steady":

> so impregnably fortressed with his own content, that
> no envious thought could ever invade his spirit: never
> surveying any man so unmeasuredly happy, whom I
> thought not justly hateful for some true impoverish-
> ment: never beholding any favour of Madam *Felicity*
> gracing another, which his well bounded content per-
> suaded not to hang in the front of his own fortune: and
> therefore as far from envying any man, as he valued
> all men infinitely distant from accomplished beatitude.[4]

He sounds like Clermont D'Ambois and, in part at least, is the

Senecal man, for it was the commonplace explanation of the behavior of satirists that they were men placed above envy, beyond the reach of Fortune's caprice. This allowed them to speak and provided motivation for their scorn. To some extent it served to explain their attitude of contempt, either by showing that they were so because, being stoics, they discarded the values of the world, or that they became stoics because it was the only recourse left them in an irrational world. But, as Chapman's efforts reveal, the passivity of the stoic, satiric or not, is difficult to dramatize. When Felice deserts his role of theoretical philosopher for one more active, his behavior is, as O. J. Campbell indicates, "not that of a stoic wrapped in measureless content, but of a malcontent, in the correct Elizabethan sense of the term —that is, of a man dissatisfied, to the point of disgust, with the entire human situation of his day."[5] Even this, however, was not enough, dramatically speaking, and Felice and his satire remain outside the action of the play. All that Marston can do is to provide a number of characters to serve as objects for Felice's satiric portraiture. Little here can be pointed to as successful dramatization of satire or as satisfactory integration of satire with a serious action.

Yet the play is suggestive of the shape of things to come. Stoicism, long ingrained in the structure of Renaissance tragedy, is given a new hold by its conjunction with the attitude of the satirist. *Antonio and Mellida* shows the possibility of blending what may be called satiric and tragic stoicism. Added to this is the idea of the Malcontent, a ready-made characterization, which, if it does not provide the stoic with a fully realized character, does give him a role that is in some degree active. He can at least concern himself with more than Clermont D'Ambois' self-congratulatory moping. Because his point of view is critical, his actions potentially subversive, the Malcontent is only a step removed from the Machiavel, as Marston was soon to discover.

It is true that Kyd had anticipated the blending of stoicism and Machiavellism in *The Spanish Tragedy,* as had Marlowe in *The Jew of Malta,* but neither dramatist had provided the philosophical basis for such a coalescence. It is only when Marston, in the interest of his satire, discovers the figure of the stoic Machiavel that the device becomes of genuine importance. In Marston's work the outlines of Webster's Machiavellian satirists, Flamineo and Bosola, first become evident.

Antonio and Mellida, however suggestive, is an imperfect play, but in its sequel, *Antonio's Revenge,* Marston progressed well beyond his rudimentary beginnings. The rhythm of *Antonio and Mellida* is broken by the satiric scenes, and Marston seems to have felt the need for a more careful integration of the satire, especially when he undertook a distinctly tragic action. His first step was to cause Felice to be murdered, and he uses this murder to set in motion his revenge plot. There is, therefore, no satirist among the characters of *Antonio's Revenge.* In his stead, the leading figures, stoics to a man, carry the burden of the satiric commentary. They are eager to discuss the satiric implication of their actions, even at the height of their tragic passion. "Why, wherefore should I weep?" says Pandulpho, Felice's father,

> Come sit, kind Nephew: come on: thou and I
> Will talk as *Chorus* to this tragedy.
> (I, v, p. 83)

The choral reflections throughout are satiric.

> O, you departed souls,
> That lodge in coffin'd trunks, which my feet press
> (If *Pythagorian Axioms* be true,
> Of spirits' transmigration) fleet no more
> To human bodies, rather live in swine,
> Inhabit wolves' flesh, scorpions', dogs', and toads',
> Rather than man. The curse of heaven rains
> In plagues unlimited through all his days.

His mature age grows only mature vice,
And ripens only to corrupt and rot
The budding hopes of infant modesty.
Still striving to be more than man, he proves
More than a devil, devilish suspect, devilish cruelty:
All hell-stray'd juice is poured to his veins,
Making him drunk with fuming surquedries,
Contempt of heaven, untam'd arrogance,
Lust, state, pride, murder.

(III, ii, p. 101)

This attempt to merge satire and tragedy produces an odd ethical result. The play is a Kydian tragedy of revenge, using the same devices and carrying essentially the same minuscule ethical significance as *The Spanish Tragedy*. It is little more than a sensational story of murder and its aftermath. Its villain is a monster, its revenge notably cruel. At the play's end, the four revengers pluck out the villain's tongue, arrange for him a Thyestean banquet, and conclude by stabbing him in mass frenzy. And all this is acted to the tune of satiric invective: "Scum of the mud of hell," "Slime of all filth," "Thou most detested toad," "Thou most retort and obtuse rascal." In the final scene the assorted revengers, with the enthusiasm of Webster's Lodovico, vie for the honor of the assassination.

Senator: Whose hand presents this gory spectacle?

Antonio: Mine.

Pandulpho: No: mine.

Alberto: No: mine.

Antonio: I will not lose the glory of the deed,
   Were all the tortures of the deepest hell
   Fix'd to my limbs. I pierc'd the monster's heart,
   With an undaunted hand.

Pandulpho: By yon bright spangled front of heaven 'twas I:
   'Twas I sluic'd out his life blood.

(V, vi, p. 131)

If these bloody cock-crows are to be taken as more than sen-
sationalistic, the revengers can be viewed only as equally monstrous with their victim. Yet such is the cumulative effect of the
satiric commentary throughout that this Machiavellian mayhem
not only is viewed with complete approval, but is generalized
into an action intended to be meaningful to all men.

Any revenger was, of necessity, something of a Machiavel,
his ways underhanded, secretive, and subversive. In the Jacobean drama he was very likely to end his life as the tragic stoic.
When Marston adds to this formidable combination the stoicism
of the satirist and integrates it crudely but inseparably with the
tragic action, he produces the earliest example in English drama
of tragic satire, the genre that Webster was to make his special
province. As a partial measure of Webster's achievement, Marston's failure in *Antonio's Revenge* is instructive.

Satiric stoicism combined readily with Machiavellism. Machiavellian activity was the obvious way of adding the essential
dramatic bite to the snarling of the verse satirist. The malignant
actions of the Machiavel could easily be conceived as an extension into deed of the bitter words of the satire. Only by such
action could the satirist in drama effect the "purge" of evildoers.
The Machiavellian satirist is related to the Vice-like character,
the "wit-intriguer," whom Jonson developed in the comical
satires on folly, as the means of leading the characters into absurdity so extreme as to cause them to leave folly entirely. But
the Machiavel is in no sense so philosophically neutral as the wit-
intriguer, whether buffoon or *homo rationalis,* Carlo or Crites.
Seeking to distinguish between the subversive activity of Hamlet
and Macbeth, a useful distinction between "good" and "bad"
Machiavellism could probably be made on the basis of its
motivation. Yet the distinction would be relative, for, to an
Elizabethan, Machiavellism was inevitably touched with evil.
It was the lust of statecraft, "savage, extreme, rude, cruel, not

to trust." Its methods carried the seeds of their own judgment, as Hamlet judges and mistrusts the methods he is forced to use when he deserts the simple way of railing for the labyrinths of Polonian intrigue. Thus it is that the satirist must become in some measure the thing he hates: Flamineo and Bosola in attacking their world must, because they are honest, mock themselves.

Marston was not so sensitive to the implications of his play in this respect as Webster was. He tried to obliterate the evil of the revengers by stressing the general ethical significance of their actions and forgetting the particulars of their deeds. The combination of Senecanism and Machiavellism with the moral revelation of satire made this possible because the satire continually directs the audience's attention away from the deed to the interpretation Marston chooses to place on it. The "choral" speeches emphasize the ethical meaning behind the action, and they tend to generalize it, to lift it from the immediate and the individual to a plane where, presumably, it will have a universal meaning. Rather as Chapman sees Clermont's revenge, Marston views the revengers' action as a model for all men to follow. The satiric reflections on the events of the play force the ethical idea into major prominence, far beyond the level of *The Spanish Tragedy,* and the concluding action presents much more than the revenge of some virtuous men on a vicious duke. It presents, astonishingly, the revenge of Virtue on Vice.

The presentation of Virtue as revenger is the result of the satirist's violent hatred of villainy—so violent that in action it becomes a kind of fanaticism, losing all sane perspective. Formal satire dealt largely with abnormalities: vicious folly, sexual aberration, Machiavellian politics, and the like. It tended, so complete was its obsession with these subjects, to cry out that what it selected to scourge was the true condition of life—that the world of its distorting vision was the world of reality. In

this respect, Marston the dramatist is not significantly different
from Marston the satirist. In *Antonio's Revenge* he is obsessed
with the figures of his own imagination, and calls them "true."
But they are not true in the sense that they are representative of
any general level of human behavior or that they figure in a
pervasive, Chapmanesque pattern of meaning. Least of all do
they have the truth that the dimensional reality of the Shakespearian characters produces. They and their problems are ab-
normal. Marston weaves a web of villainy and cries, This is the
way life is! But it needs no ghost from the grave to tell us that
the world of *Antonio's Revenge* bears as little resemblance to the
world of human action as does the world of *The Spanish Tragedy*.

What really has happened? Is it only that Marston has not
represented on his stage the variety of human experience? If
so, Webster cannot be said to have done better. Indeed, Webster's severest critics have found much the same fault with his
tragedies as has here been suggested about *Antonio's Revenge*.
Since he too adds satire to his tragic pattern, he risks the danger
of the same ethical confusion that overtakes Marston. It is true
that Webster is obsessed with his vision, and it is a vision of evil
closer by far to Marston's than to Chapman's. And, like Marston, Webster calls this vision the true condition of life and
generalizes from the particular story to a wider human scene.
Yet there is a difference. Of the writer of tragedy it is not enough
to ask, What more can he do than seek truth with his own eyes?
Light changes and the shapes of things vary: Chapman's noon
and Webster's twilight do not reveal the same world. This the
tragic artist must know and take into account. It is not his vision
of the facts that counts, so much as his vision beyond the facts.
"Tragedy," in Lewis Galantière's phrase, "is clean, it is firm, it is
flawless,"[6] and it can be so only if the vision beyond the fact is
clear. The tragic writer is not thereby permitted to turn away
from the apparent realities of his world, however sickening they

may be. But he must remember that external truth is variable, and it is never all. It is the chaos to which second vision brings order. It provides the elements to be arranged in the flawless design.

It is precisely here that Webster is startlingly different from Marston, even as he appears to share Marston's primary vision of the world. Let it be granted momentarily that the world can be as evil as Marston saw it. Let the charge of melodramatic sensationalism be dropped. It still remains that Marston's final vision, which is called a vision of good and which posits a restoration of order, is a vision of evil more sensational than anything else in the play. The triumph of the satiric Machiavel is the triumph of anarchy, not order, and Marston did not know it! He was betrayed by his satiric obsession into taking the "horrible example" of satire as the whole truth, the aberrational, the monstrous as the total complex of the world. This is forgivable, but what cannot be forgiven is his failure to see that his concluding action is a part of the thing scourged. It is not the result of a farther vision of ultimate order. In the end, Marston offers as his tragic good the very thing that his satire has proved to be evil. He thereby distorts both the satiric and the tragic truth of his action, and no course is left him but to voice the satirist's cry for the complete destruction of the human scene, the full opening of the floodgate: "'Twas I sluic'd out his life blood."

The result of such severe distortion is that, although Marston's plays are always interesting, rarely diffuse or shapeless, their highest emotion is one of bitterness, their most exalted mood, one of disillusion. His greatest work, *The Malcontent,* attains only the level of tragicomedy. The full tragic perception is blinded by the harsher light of satire. Webster, more sensitive to his own implications, more able dramatically, found the way to blend satire and tragedy so that, from the combination of genres, and in spite of a vision of evil more obsessive than Marston's, the truth proper to tragedy could emerge.

Tragedy and Satire

To write tragedy that is also satire presents, on the face of it, an almost insoluble problem. For tragedy depends on belief in the fullest potential spiritual achievement of man. Because the potential is unrealized in any world, the tragic ideal must carry with it some of the evanescence of illusion. But it is the especial power of tragedy that it tests the capabilities of men by the strength of their faith in the ideal. Pity, to be sure, lies in the spectacle of a man's world shattering about him, and there is terror in the sense of godlike capabilities wasted by the death of a tragic hero. But his heroism—and indeed the greatness of tragedy—lies in his triumphant assertion of faith in the potentialities of man's spirit, whatever the condition of the mortal world. Illusory these powers may be in the world of the audience, but tragedy must prove them real and make the case for their value.

The essential difference between satire and tragedy may simply be that satire is not required to make such a case, positively. It may offer its ideal condition by the implication of strong negative statement. It does not have to prove the ideal by displaying it in action in a world that temporarily is to be taken as reality. The ideal that satire sets, either for individual men or their society, tends to be left abstractly cold, or made somewhat wistfully a part of the background. Frequently it is all but hidden under an avalanche of mockery. Satire, like tragedy, knows pity and terror, for it too concerns itself with man's spiritual potential and with man in "actuality," surrounded by the limiting bonds of the flesh. But whereas tragedy attempts to bring the two together, satire measures the gulf between, finding in such measurement material for mockery. The tragic hero must strive to partake of both. Satire can only laugh or cry at his attempts; in either event it must reveal the pretensions of his faith. The essential bitterness of satire lies in the sickening sense of disillusion that comes from proving the faith of tragedy to be illusory. To the satirist, the tragic conditions are those of failure; to the tragedian, they are those of triumph.

This may explain why it is virtually impossible to merge the points of view of satirist and tragedian.[7] It is not that tragedy can make no use of satire. Shakespeare uses the tone and techniques of the satirist in portraying the malcontent Hamlet and the mad Lear. O. J. Campbell is right when he states,

> The uncontrollable impulse to mock reveals the inner chaos into which the doomed creatures seek desperately . . . to bring order. Much of the bitterness with which Shakespeare fills his later tragedies and much of the sharpness of the inner conflicts which these plays reveal are then the result of the poet's development of a traditional satiric character [i.e., the malcontent]. Both are the product of the scornful spirit of derision which reflects the malcontent's exasperation with life.[8]

Yet, the disillusionment revealed by the satiric commentary of Hamlet or Lear is only a part of that which must be overcome in the hero's upward thrust from despair to faith, from "To me, what is this quintessence of dust?" to "There's a divinity that shapes our ends . . ." In these tragedies it is the tragic hero, not Shakespeare, who assumes the satiric point of view, and the hero's early vision of the world is blotted out by his ultimate statement of faith. Shakespeare brings the tragic and satiric together by making the satire part of the plot, and eliminating it from the final vision. The satiric point of view is never the final position of judgment in the tragedies.

Other dramatists were less able in their attempted fusion. It has already been noted that Marston tended to call the objects of the satirist's obsessed and perverted view the true condition of life. The result was to make tragedy impossible and to leave in its stead a crabbed, dominantly melodramatic spectacle whose ethical signification is at best obscure. *The Revenger's Tragedy,* to take another example, has in it the materials of true tragic spectacle. Vendici, like the Shakespearian heroes, is struggling to find some basis for asserting faith in mankind. Yet Tourneur's excoriation of the world he creates is so extensive and so convincing, even in its enormity, that ultimately he finds Vendici as corrupt as the world he lives in. In the end, Vendici accepts his action as evil and views himself in the same executioner's spirit as he viewed the torchlight processional with which the play opens. Tourneur is left with only the vestigial reminders of pity and the terrifying anarchy of despair. The positive power of tragedy is not present.

Not so with Webster. In the second part of *Tamburlaine,* one of the conqueror's "lovely boys" vows, as a demonstration of filial piety, that he would swim through a sea of blood to reach his father's throne. This is a curiously apt image for Webster's achievement. The other writers of tragic satire drowned in that sea, but Webster reached the throne. It would be easy to say that he did so because he was a greater poet, but Marston and Tourneur were poets of no mean strength. It was not his words alone that saved Webster. He was saved by his sensitivity to the thematic complexities of the combination of Senecan, Machiavel, and stoic satirist, and by his ability, as a dramatist, to solve the technical problems arising from the juxtaposition of tragedy and satire.

CHAPTER FIVE

SATIRIC COUNTERPOINT *to the* TRAGIC ACTION

IN WEBSTERIAN TRAGEDY a vision of man as he might be is held in steady focus with the view of man as he is. The result is a unique counterpointing of tragedy and satire. The individuals Webster chose for his tragic story would, a few years earlier, have provided the brightest evidence of man's potential greatness. His dukes and duchesses, the splendid men and women of the Italian Renaissance, were tributes to the glory of mankind. In his study of the reality of their glory, Webster saw that much about it was sham, but that even yet they could stand as great specimens of humanity. Their heroic quality, their capacity for magnificent struggle in the assertion of their individuality, made them fit subjects for the heightened action of tragedy.

The tragedies, however, are concerned not only with vigorous individualistic action. They show also the pernicious inroads which the world of actuality makes on the lives of the heroic protagonists. Consequently, the heightened action is subjected to unrelenting satirical analysis, designed to reveal the full meaning of individualistic action in its relation to society and to exhibit the heroic for what it is in terms common to all mankind. The contemporary allusions and the details of local color only serve to emphasize the presence of the actual in the heroic world.

By exhibiting his action from two points of view, Webster could show not only how splendid individuals can be, ideally, but also to what they are brought in actuality. Man, the satire shows, even at his most willful is not the master of his fate. His power is restricted by death; disease limits his body; the wrath of men and the laws of society check him in his course. However heroic, the protagonists of Websterian tragedy are, in Donne's phrase, "involved in *Mankind,*" and this the satire never forgets.

In making the tragic story the object of his satire, Webster was creating a difficult imaginative and technical problem for himself. The satiric and the heroic elements had to be held in balance, for each had within it that which could destroy the other. Conceivably, the heroic story could have proved so moving as to nullify the stringent effects of the satiric comment; or, more probably, the latter would have destroyed the heightening necessary to the achievement of tragedy. That Webster maintained a balance between the two is a tribute to his control of his medium. Most of the Jacobean satirical tragedies did not achieve the heightening indispensable for the full tragic effect, because they were not conceived with sufficient imaginative amplitude to escape abasement under the weight of the satire. Satire in Tourneur, for instance, dampens almost all glow of tragedy. Webster, however, was equal to the problem imaginatively, and satire, though it marked the tragic flight, could not bring it to earth.

Webster realized that there was still a glory about life, however stained it appeared. Especially there was grandeur in the capacity of individuals to struggle to maintain their integrity. Since integrity of life was the one thing which the forces of oppression and mortality could not shatter, its retention was valuable in itself. Satire, therefore, could reveal nothing rotten about either the capacity for struggle or the preservation of integrity. These great qualities alone in men were not illusion.

All other values might be called in question, but these escaped
the devastation of the satirical analysis. Significantly, it was on
integrity of life that Webster placed the emphasis of his heroic
story. It does not matter, in the end, when death wells over
Webster's stage, that the struggle has brought no lasting good.
In integrity and in the struggle to preserve it, there has been an
affirmation despite the end, despite evil, despite the knowledge
that the world is moribund and rotten—a fit subject for cruel,
satirical analysis.

Webster's sensitive and complex handling of his tragic themes
will be discussed in the final chapter. First, however, it is necessary to detail the techniques by which Webster managed to produce in his audience both the objective point of view necessary
to satire and the surrender of disbelief required by tragedy.
Marston, relying on explicit choral interpretation of the action
by his leading characters, managed to nullify both his satire and
his tragedy. He created the impression of aware men who yet did
not understand their own actions. Technically, Webster did better than this. To be sure, he used explicit interpretation of the
action, perhaps more than Marston did. His *sententiae* and
moral fables provide examples of this, and there is also much
direct choral statement of a satiric kind. But for the most part
the explicit devices are motivated in character and, more often
than not, seem dramatically appropriate. Furthermore, the
satiric commentary is carried implicitly along with the tragic
story, thus making the satiric vision pervasive from the audience's
point of view as well as from the characters'. This dramatic integration of satire and tragedy Webster accomplishes by contrasting two actions, one of which serves to reveal the enormity of
events in the other, and again by developing through his imagery
a tone that runs counter to the dominant action of the scene.
These methods of integration help to create a compelling dramatic experience, and prevent, as Marston's simple explicitness

did not prevent, the audience from judging the characters by an objective standard which neither tragedy nor satire can support.

Sententia and Fable

The suspicion with which contemporary audiences look on easy moralizing has led them to register distaste for the *sententiae* which abound in the early drama. The sententious couplet, however, was a source of pleasure to Webster's first audiences, and even today the *sententia* can obtain fine dramatic results. Sententious statements as Webster uses them are direct comments on the action, and serve as agents of the satire. They represent the dramatist's point of view by making a generalized statement to point the significance of a speech or a scene. Although they tend to lose the harsh tone of the formal verse satirists, they retain the satiric awareness of the discrepancy between appearance and reality.

Webster wrote them beautifully:

> Both flowers and weeds, spring when the Sun is warm,
> And great men do great good, or else great harm.
> ### (*WD*, II, ii, 55)

"Whether we fall by ambition, blood, or lust,
"Like Diamonds, we are cut with our own dust.
(*DM*, V, v, 91)

The sententious couplet serves the drama as well as the satire only if it is integrated into the action in such a way as to make its point without causing the audience to lose commitment with the narrative. Webster, although he occasionally appears to be using the *sententiae* for their own sakes, usually makes them serve the purpose of characterization at the same time as they subtly define the action.

At Cornelia's first entrance in *The White Devil*, for instance, the couplet gives her an immediate, almost complete characterization. Brachiano's amorous blandishments reach their height, and suddenly Cornelia steps forward from her hiding place like a prophetess:

> *Brachiano:*   . . . you shall to me at once,
>   Be Dukedom, health, wife, children, friends and all.
> *Cornelia:* Woe to light hearts!—they still forerun our fall!
>   (I, ii, 257)

The stern words, chiming against Brachiano's promises, define the inflexible moral roots of Cornelia's character. Her subsequent speech of "grim reproof" does not characterize her more completely than these words, which gain unusual strength from the couplet construction. As Rupert Brooke noted, the couplet has "a Greek ring about it."[1]

But Webster did not let it go at this. A few lines later, Cornelia cries out,

> The lives of Princes should like dials move,
> Whose regular example is so strong,
> They make the times by them go right or wrong.
>   (I, ii, 279)

By now the audience will accept the *sententia* as appropriate to Cornelia's character, but here, more than in her first words, it will accept her as an agent of the satire, for her lines manifest the satiric point of view toward the clandestine meeting of the lovers. Webster had created in the darkened room a scene of sinister beauty. Zanche spreads the stage with a carpet and "two fair Cushions." Vittoria relates her dream of the yew, Brachiano takes her in his arms, and at this point Cornelia bursts in. A moment is taken to establish her personal character and then, significantly, she stresses the aberration between Brachiano's duty as a prince and his present conduct, rather than the dishonor done to her house. The scene is stripped of its surface luxury and shown for what it is: the assignation of a degenerate prince with an immoral woman. Cornelia's emphasis is both bitterly personal and generally satiric.

By including in his plays such extensive set pieces as the moral fables, Webster was doubtless indulging his copybook habit at the risk of the progress of his dramas. The fable, however, is only a step removed from such fine dramatic passages as Vittoria's dream of the yew and Monticelso's "Character of a Whore." And, as with the *sententia,* when the fable is not presented for its own sake but seems to develop from the action it becomes a serviceable theatrical instrument for satiric commentary.

At the end of the great quarrel between Vittoria and Brachiano in the House of Convertites, Flamineo tells his master the fable of the bird that picks the worms from the crocodile's teeth. The "fish" refuses to reward the bird for its service, and "that the bird may not talk largely of her abroad for non-payment," clamps shut its jaws with the intention of swallowing the bird. The bird, however, is armed by nature with a quill on its head, "top o'th' which wounds the crocodile i'th' mouth." The wounded crocodile opens its chaps, "and away flies the pretty tooth-picker from her cruel patient."[2]

The application and the appropriateness of the fable are clear. Flamineo tells it as a warning to Brachiano against ingratitude. Shortly before this, he and Brachiano have quarreled seriously. Flamineo knows that princes can alter their favors to punishment at the least annoyance, and dares not jeopardize his chance of reward by threatening Brachiano outright. At the same time, he does not intend to let his master forget him. Consequently, he veils his threat in a fable, and, when he is taxed for an explanation, produces an impromptu application of the fable, pretending that it is a warning to Vittoria against ingratitude to her lover. But the real meaning is apparent and Flamineo's point is made. The fable is thus integrated into character and situation.

As comment, the fable is especially significant, since the lines

that immediately precede it are a promise of reward from Brachiano:

> . . . follow me. ·
> I will advance you all: for you *Vittoria,*
> Think of a Duchess' title.

(IV, ii, 221)

Later, Webster, wishing to show the folly of trusting in courtly
promises, uses as an example Brachiano's failure to keep this
promise. It is necessary for him to underscore the promise with
a comment that will suggest the course of later action. The fable
of the crocodile's ingratitude makes the comment directly. Not
only is the fable integrated into the dramatic story, but it provides a satiric interpretation of the action by emphasizing the
discrepancy between a prince's promises and his rewards.

Choral Comment

Another method of juxtaposing comment and action is by choral
comment from one or more characters. It is one of the simplest
ways of bringing out the desired satiric interpretation, as Marston discovered. The individual with an objective point of view,
allowed to make realistic observations concerning those about
him, was no stranger to Elizabethan drama. He is the stoic
Felice; he is the malcontent Malevole; he is the wit-intriguer
Macilente; he is the revenger Vendici; he is the man of common
sense, Enobarbus; and once, sublimely, he is a nameless Fool.
Not always is he used for satiric purposes, but in Websterian
tragedy, where objectivity is an integral part of his character,
he is the chief singer of the satiric descant.

Flamineo and Bosola in this one respect bear a striking resemblance to such figures as Macilente and Carlo Buffone in *Every
Man Out of His Humour*. They have the same cynical spirit,
the scorn and raillery of the earlier *raisonneurs*. But Webster

makes it clear that this satiric spirit is part of their characters. Both Flamineo and Bosola have ample cause for disillusion. They are Renaissance forgotten men. They have neither security nor hope. Their hunger is barely satisfied by other men's favors, their better natures not at all. Too well acquainted with the evil in man, they see him as a creature without glory; their disillusioned gaze strips him of splendor. The scorn of satire comes easily to their lips. As an audience would doubtless recognize, their railing commentary is completely motivated by their characters.

Webster's outstanding use of direct choral comment occurs in the scene between Brachiano, Vittoria, and Flamineo in the House of Convertites. Brachiano loses his head when he finds a letter which Francisco has written Vittoria. He flares into a jealous rage, calls her whore, and casts her from him. Vittoria, seeing it is of little use to deny his accusations, attacks him with such verbal violence that he capitulates. But Vittoria will have none of him. She throws herself on the bed, weeping, and will not listen to his attempts to win her back. Flamineo, whose hopes for preferment rest on the continuance of Brachiano's favor to Vittoria and her family, begins a ribald commentary, designed both as a styptic to Vittoria's rage and a stimulant to Brachiano's desire. Webster uses it further as the satiric point of reference for the quarrel.

Brachiano and Vittoria speak with the tongues of heroes:

> *Brachiano:*   Wilt thou hear me?
> Once to be jealous of thee is t'express
> That I will love thee everlastingly,
> And never more be jealous.
>
> *Vittoria:*   O thou fool,
> Whose greatness hath by much o'ergrown thy wit!
> What dar'st thou do, that I not dare to suffer,
> Excepting to be still thy whore? for that . . .

> In the sea's bottom sooner thou shalt make
> A bonfire.
> > (IV, ii, 142)

At this point Flamineo interrupts with a satirical yawn: "O, no oaths for god's sake!" His language is full of scurrility, playing a scatological serenade to the lovers on the bed.

> What a damn'd impostume is a woman's will!
> Can nothing break it? fie, fie, my Lord.
> Women are caught as you take Tortoises,
> She must be turn'd on her back. Sister, by this hand
> I am on your side. Come, come, you have wrong'd her
> What a strange credulous man were you, my Lord,
> To think the Duke of Florence would love her!
> Will any Mercer take another's ware
> When once 't is tows'd and sullied? And yet, sister,
> How scurvily this frowardness becomes you! . . .
> > A quiet woman
> Is a still water under a great bridge.
> A man may shoot her safely. . . .
> Stop her mouth, with a sweet kiss, my Lord
> So—now the tide's turned the vessel's come about.
> He's a sweet armful. O we curl'd-hair'd men
> Are still most kind to women. This is well. . . .
> O, sir, your little chimneys
> Do ever cast most smoke. I sweat for you.
> Couple together with as deep a silence,
> As did the Grecians in their wooden horse.
> > (IV, ii, 152, 203)

As satiric comment, Flamineo's words are designed to show what underlies the "grand passion." There is to be no illusion about this love affair, no glossing of its causes or its manifestations. Yet this is not Cornelia speaking; no social condemnation is intended. It is necessary only that the terms of the love affair be made clear, and this the very enormity of Flamineo's remarks easily accomplishes.

Evidently Flamineo has excellent reasons for talking as he does. The commentary is thoroughly integrated into the dramatic sequence. But there is another technical problem to be considered here. The *sententia* and the fable, so long as they do not interfere with the audience's suspension of disbelief, are in no danger of affecting the heroic action of the tragic story. As satiric comment, they serve as passing reminders of a point of view which the author wishes to maintain. They are not powerful enough in themselves to dominate an emotional tragic action. Flamineo's comments about Vittoria and Brachiano are, in their extent and vividness, quite another matter, and it may well be asked whether or not his lines debase tragedy to the level of bedroom farce.

To prevent such a possibility, Webster does not alter the tenor of his satire, but adjusts, instead, the tone of the tragic story. The quarrel begins with some of the most notable lines in the play. In his rage, Brachiano cries out to Vittoria,

> Your beauty! ô, ten thousand curses on't.
> How long have I beheld the devil in crystal!
> Thou hast led me, like a heathen sacrifice,
> With music, and with fatal yokes of flowers
> To my eternal ruin. Woman to man
> Is either a God or a wolf.
>   (IV, ii, 88)

This is the poetry of tragedy, the heightened dialogue of heroic emotion. But, as Brachiano's rage spends itself, a subtle change takes place. Vittoria is silent, awaiting an opening. When it comes, nothing can stop her. She hales Brachiano with her tongue, forcing him to forget his rage, apologize, and woo her to him. Her lines are a curious mixture of the masculine fury she displayed at the trial and a thoroughly feminine display of temperament. Mingled with the heroic dialogue are lines like these:

> What do you call this house?
> Is this your palace? did not the Judge style it

A house of penitent whores? who sent me to it?
Who hath the honour to advance *Vittoria*
To this incontinent college? is't not you?
Is't not your high preferment? Go, go brag
How many Ladies you have undone, like me.
Fare you well Sir; let me hear no more of you.

(IV, ii, 114)

The quarrel has, from the moment of Brachiano's capitulation
to Vittoria, come off the heroic level on which it began. Webster
emphasizes, in the latter part of the scene, his heroine's womanliness, an aspect of her character which has thus far not been
revealed in detail. Brachiano cannot control or understand her,
and her riggish behavior throws him temporarily off his dignity.
His awkward efforts to still the tempest he has raised are realistic, even amusing, and they effectively lower the tone of the tragic
action so that the commentary is in no danger of causing it to
appear pompous or absurd. By emphasizing Vittoria's womanliness, Webster quite properly lets Flamineo stress the sexual
aspects of the love affair in his frank analysis.

Again, at the death of Brachiano, choral comment is used to
direct the attention to certain aspects of the scene, and here it is
integrated with the action in such a way as to permit intensifica-
tion rather than diminution of the tragic situation. Part of Webster's intention was to show the perfunctory way in which princes
were mourned. Brachiano at his moment of triumph is poisoned
by Francisco, Lodovico, and Gasparo, who have entered his
court in disguise. As Brachiano realizes he is dying, he with-
draws into his cabinet. Flamineo and the disguised Francisco
have the stage. Without more ado for the dying man, Flamineo
remarks, "To see what solitariness is about dying Princes!" With
the callous objectivity of a satirist, he predicts that the tears shed
for Brachiano will be dry within a few hours. His own failure to
mourn his lord is the result of Brachiano's refusal to reward him,

and he explains to Francisco how readily he would have cozened Brachiano had he found the opportunity.

Again, the matter-of-fact objectivity with which Flamineo views all things makes its mark. Not a little of the effectiveness of the comment lies in the callousness of the speaker. To the audience, Flamineo stands as a living example of his own state-ment: he proves that a prince dies unmourned. The choral com-ment is rooted in character, and the episode achieves force from its very enormity. Brachiano's words before his exit have been carefully chosen to create the maximum sympathy for him. There may not be tears, but when he cries out for Vittoria,

> Where's this good woman? had I infinite worlds
> They were too little for thee. Must I leave thee?
>
> (V, iii, 18)

the audience, by virtue of its sympathy for Vittoria at least, will recognize some goodness in the man, and feel strongly the ele-ment of horror in his death. The consequent effect of Flamineo's commentary, which follows immediately on Brachiano's

> On pain of death, let no man name death to me,
> It is a word infinitely terrible—
>
> (V, iii, 39)

is not difficult to imagine. The audience will protest not only against Flamineo's callous behavior but against the "solitariness" that attends a prince in his death. The horror of the tragic story is increased by the direct application of satiric commentary.

In such scenes as these, Webster integrated moral precept and choral commentary as well as any dramatist could do. Yet, how-ever well motivated in character such evaluation is, its explicit nature tends to set it a little outside or apart from the action of the play. The methods thus far described are an improvement on, but not essentially different from, the techniques developed by Marston. But Webster found other ways of bringing satiric evaluation within the structure of the tragic world. By the juxtaposition of two contrasting actions and by the contrast of action and tone within a scene, he made satiric judgment an essential part of the response to his tragedy.

Contrasting Action

Contrasting action is a structural axiom of Elizabethan and Jacobean drama. It is used everywhere, for every conceivable purpose, from comedy to tragedy, from vagaries of romance in *Friar Bacon and Friar Bungay* to dramas of wide-ranging psychological implication in *The Changeling*. Nowhere else, however, is it used so consistently for satiric purposes as in Websterian tragedy. Webster uses it to stress, as satire should, the wide distance and, at the same time, the frightening interplay between good and evil, the pitiable and the horrible in society. Vicious action is scaled against gentle; in the starkness of the contrast, both are stripped of appearances, and the essential quality of each is intensified.

Examples in both tragedies are plentiful: in *The White Devil*, Giovanni's grief for his mother is played against the apparent heroism of Vittoria's behavior in the arraignment scene; the conspiracy of Francisco and the murder of Marcello undercut the triumph of Brachiano and of Flamineo; there is the scene in Brachiano's death chamber between his murderer and the lascivious Moorish maid; there is Flamineo's mock massacre, soon to be followed by the reality of the triple murders.

In *The Duchess of Malfi*, the ideality of Antonio's opening statement about the French court is followed by scenes designed to show the ugliness of the present reality. The harshness of the Aragonian brothers' diatribe against their sister's remarriage is contrasted with the charm and quiet of the proposal scene. This in turn gives way to the scenes of the Duchess' pregnancy, and again the satire dispels the illusion of greatness. At the end of the tragedy, after the murder of Julia and just before the final carnage, Webster pauses to allow the Duchess' voice to sound gently from her tomb, and the contrast again aids in revealing the essential nature of the surrounding scenes of violence.

Webster, though he makes no direct satiric comment in these juxtaposed scenes, is indirectly expressing an attitude by emphasizing the very enormity of the contrast. Part of the horror of the tragedies is that extremes of virtuous and vicious behavior are found close together in the tragic world. This is, in the satiric context of the plays, a satiric perception. It reveals, as the formal satire earlier had revealed, the pervasiveness of evil, which corrupts the fairest show and runs as a turbulent undercurrent below the golden surface of life. It suggests that there is no escape from the essential ugliness which the satirist has set himself to reveal. And, more important to the success of the tragedies, this revelation cannot be denied, as explicit satiric comment could be denied in Marston. It is a part of the structure of the tragic world; it is essential to the vision of experience the spectators are asked to share. When satiric comment is integrated into tragedy in this way, there is no danger of its destroying the rhythm of the play or shattering the dramatic mood. Each episode, by virtue of its contrast to scenes preceding or succeeding it, becomes comment in itself. The contrast serves not only to intensify the dramatic tensions of the juxtaposed scenes but to give the audience the desired perspective on the tragic action.

Contrasting Tone

Another technique for blending comment with action is the creation of a tonal quality which is in contrast with the action of the scene. In the two tragedies the evocations of imagery, subject matter, and vocabulary often run counter to the events in the scene, suggesting a perspective which the action alone will not reveal. In the proposal scene which concludes the first act of *The Duchess of Malfi,* the action is quiet, even charming. In the thoughts of the man and woman there is no suggestion of evil or madness or death. The world for them does not exist outside the circumference of their love. Yet the audience cannot forget, cannot lose its perspective even for so short a time. The ironies contingent upon satiric revelation can never be relaxed. And so the Duchess speaks of making her will, of "deep groans, and terrible ghastly looks" of men on their deathbeds, of winding sheets, of equivocations, violent passions, riddles and dreams, of her statue carved in alabaster, kneeling by her husband's tomb. Antonio's imagery refers to blindness, and devils, and to marriage as heaven or hell. He is indeed prophetic of the Duchess' end when he says,

> Ambition (Madam) is a great man's madness,
> That is not kept in chains, and close-pent-rooms,
> But in fair lightsome lodgings, and is girt
> With the wild noise of prattling visitants,
> Which makes it lunatic, beyond all cure.

> (I, i, 483)

"Fear" and "pity" are recurrent words. The Duchess describes their marriage as a "sacred Gordian," whose doom, as F. L. Lucas points out, "was no other than to be severed by a sword."[3] None of this, be it noted, is sufficient to destroy the beauty of the scene, yet it suggests a deeper, more terrifying reality at the precise moment that the play reaches its highest lyric point. The satire is present in the orchestration, suggesting what will later be shown, the intertwining of sex and death, and madness yet to come.

In the following scenes the effect is repeated. The disgusting imagery which pervades the scenes of the Duchess' pregnancy forces the audience to be aware of the physical aspects of the pregnant woman. Bosola's description of her is revolting.

> I observe our Duchess
> Is sick a days, she pukes, her stomach seethes,
> The fins of her eye-lids look most teeming blue,
> She wanes i'th'cheek, and waxes fat i'th'flank;
> And (contrary to our *Italian* fashion,)
> Wears a loose-bodied Gown—
>
> (II, i, 65)

But the pregnant woman deserves better than this. With life rising in her, she is not emblematic of decay or of death. Normally, she should represent a kind of human spring, for in her vitality is reborn and continued. Earlier, she and Antonio have compared themselves to "the loving Palms . . . That nev'r bore fruit divided." And in the pregnancy scene the conception of fertility remains. "I have bought some Apricocks," Bosola says, "The first our Spring yields." Yet in this world the yield of springtime, the fertile continuity of life, cannot survive. If by no other agency than human greed, it too must be contaminated by decay. Of the apricots, Bosola says,

> I forgot to tell you the knave Gardener,
> (Only to raise his profit by them the sooner)
> Did ripen them in horse-dung.
>
> (II, i, 148)

The beauty of the woman is destroyed with the image, and Bosola's satire stands.

Webster wished to show two qualities about the Duchess: she had in her the dangerous "spirit of woman"; and she could assert the integrity of her life when all else had been taken from her. The satire suggested in the images here serves both purposes. The spirit of woman is first revealed in the Duchess' hysterical behavior during her pregnancy. When the audience had last seen her, she was the great lady of her court and the desirable woman of the proposal scene. Now Bosola begins to attack her greatness and beauty and to prepare the audience for what is to come. His revolting imagery is an affront to the Duchess' person and a prelude to the intensive satiric mortification which is to come in the fourth act. There, being forced to contemplate the loathsomeness of her body is part of her torture. Bosola's words here mark the beginning of the later revelation. His images achieve their satiric effectiveness by forming a disgusting tonal sheath for the idealistic portrayal which has been presented thus far.

In the skillful integration of satiric comment with tragic narrative, by the *sententia* and the fable, by direct choral comment, by the contrast of two actions, and in the contrast of tone and action, Webster reveals himself to be a master of the dramatic medium. Only rarely did he yield to the temptation to include preceptual statement extraneous to the action. His tragedies are, for the most part, successful dramatizations of both the satiric and tragic points of view. Because of this double vision, the plays have a plasticity which many tragedies of the time seem to lack. They never fail to arouse emotion; they never seem unrelated to reality. In this respect, Websterian tragedy makes its statement about life as powerfully as dramas which have an explicitly stated thematic content ever can.

But technical achievement is only one aspect of the problem. Marston's failure in *Antonio's Revenge* was in part a technical one, but in the main it resulted from his inability to perceive fully the implications of his own statements, either as satirist or as tragedian. Here, in his sensitive and courageous response to the world of his vision, Webster's full stature as the second tragic dramatist of England is seen. To assess him in this capacity it is necessary to investigate in detail the thematic statement in both tragedies: this alone can reveal how he transformed the conventions of dramatic satire into a profoundly tragic comment on the life of man.

CHAPTER SIX

THE SATIRIC PANORAMA

"The skull beneath the skin"

WEBSTER, T. S. ELIOT SAID, "was much possessed by death"; he was also possessed by life—a spectacle of physical and moral horror from which he could not turn away. Compelled to stare in morbid fascination, unable to resolve the problems which he clearly saw, Webster in his two great tragedies demonstrated that he at least had the courage of his vision. He struggled to find a philosophical basis that might enable him to image the world as part of a coherent scheme, but in this he failed, for he was too intimately concerned with that world ever to achieve the detachment necessary to Chapman's "heightened style." Rather he reacted with a frenetic emotional response, part revulsion, part sympathy, and he seems to have resolved to set down as truthfully as he could the causes of his pity and contempt, feeling perhaps that in a truthful redaction of human behavior he could find a pattern of explanation. He tried in numerous didactic passages to explain and offer remedy for the suffering of men, but, ultimately, his honesty rendered his commentary ineffective. The problems were beyond specifically ethical solution, and Webster lacked confidence in didactic guidance. Although he often adhered to traditional moral distinctions, he was apparently unable to discover an acceptable system for the evaluation of good and evil.

The reasons for this have been partly explored in the analysis of the tragic action, but the problem may be stated more broadly, that its satiric as well as its tragic implications may be seen. What (Webster asks) is the value of life in a decaying world, where men by oppression and disease are brought relentlessly to death? What appears evil descends surely to death, but so, just as surely, does good. In death they become the same, and in life their evaluation is fraught with confusion. The virtuous gain no reward, and Webster feels only pity for them. Good to no avail is of no value. Yet evil is as difficult to judge. Antisocial behavior is so dominant as to become almost the norm of the on-stage world. Webster continually equates it with the natural rot of the body and sees it as an inescapable, often impersonal force rather than as the product of remediable human action. Abstracted from its human origins, it becomes difficult to appraise beyond the evaluation involved in the mere recognition of its presence. Added to this is the bewildering mixture of good and evil in the same person—in Vittoria, Brachiano, Flamineo, Bosola, even, in Webster's terms, the Duchess herself. Life, as it appears to Webster, is a moral chaos. Ultimately, no clarifying philosophy is possible, for man's mortality renders meaningless the very terms on which such a philosophy must be based.

Unable to find a solution to the problems he raises, and yet unable to effect a compromise with the terrifying world of his vision, Webster tries to present the ugliness beneath the artificial glory. Every character of importance, every situation, the noblest ethical statement in both tragedies is attacked by Webster's relentless analysis. His entire energy is directed toward teaching man "Wherein he is imperfect." Yet this was done without any clear hope of making man perfect, for perfection was meaningless, "a bare name, and no essential thing." As exorcisers of illusion, the plays present to men the falsity and folly of their lives. Possibly Webster hoped his work would arouse men to a concern for their world, but beyond the representation of the truth as he saw it, he could not progress. None of his recommendations for remedial action have ultimate validity in the tragic action, and, as a result, the plays remain grim object lessons in the same sense that Yorick's skull was an object lesson to Hamlet. They cut through platitude and delusion to the fact of death. From the facing of the fact in its bareness, Hamlet came to an acceptance of all that lay ahead. Webster, characteristically, remained by the open grave.

"Courtly reward and punishment"

The opening scene in *The White Devil* states the theme of the play: the evils of courtly reward and punishment.

> *Lodovico:* Banish'd!
> *Antonelli:*   It griev'd me much to hear the sentence.
> *Lodovico:* Ha, Ha, ô *Democritus* thy Gods
>   That govern the whole world! Courtly reward
>   And punishment.
> (I, i, 1)

The rest of the scene is concerned with the development of this statement and the establishment of the theme. Lodovico has been banished, and his friends Gasparo and Antonelli attempt to calm him by pointing out that there was some justice in the sentence. They join in one of Webster's accusatory duets and try to show Lodovico the error of his prodigal way of life in Rome. But Lodovico counters their assertions by asking what justice there is in his punishment when greater criminals go untouched, and such men as the Duke of Brachiano, who "by close panderism seeks to prostitute / The honour of *Vittoria Corombona,*" are permitted to remain in Rome. Is this the reward of service? It would have been better to have been condemned to death. He concludes,

This is the world's alms; pray make use of it—
Great men sell sheep thus, to be cut in pieces,
When first they have shorn them bare and sold their fleeces.

(I, i, 60)

During Lodovico's lament and his friends' remonstrances, the larger theme, which is styled "courtly reward and punishment," is divided into three parts for later development: first, the rotten prodigality of court life; second, the evils of a social system in which sycophants flatter a lord for an uncertain living; third, the treachery of a prince's capricious "justice." These are the chief aspects of the theme which appear in action and comment throughout the play, and Webster never loses sight of them. Indeed, at the very end, Vittoria and Flamineo, dying, speak words that bear home these ideas.

Vittoria: O happy they that never saw the Court,
"Nor ever knew great Man but by report.
                              Vittoria dies.

Flamineo: . . . Let all that belong to Great men remember
th' old wives' tradition, to be like the Lions i'th' Tower
on Candlemas day, to mourn if the Sun shine, for fear
of the pitiful remainder of winter to come.

(V, vi, 261, 268)

Thus, at the last moment in the life of his tragic heroine, Webster restates the theme that he set forth in the opening of the play.[1]

Between the preliminary statement and the final summation, Webster develops the aspects of courtly reward and punishment as they were defined at the outset.

The corruption and extravagance of court life are constantly in evidence. Cornelia interrupts the lavishly staged assignation of her daughter and Brachiano and makes explicit their lascivious wickedness. When she and Flamineo are left alone, their dialogue widens the thematic implications of the exemplary scene just played. Flamineo turns on his mother in a rage that she should interfere with his hopes for preferment. How, he asks, can one be virtuous, when one is at the mercy of a corrupt world? Why must he resort to pandering his sister except that his father's prodigality consumed his estate and left him penniless? What has he learned in his university days and in his experience at court?

> Conspiring with a beard
> Made me a Graduate—then to this Duke's service—
> I visited the Court, whence I return'd
> More courteous, more lecherous by far,
> But not a suit the richer.
> (I, ii, 316)

Such statements early in the play serve to fix in the minds of the audience the corruption of the court. The succeeding episodes of brawling, treachery, lust, and murder all become exemplifications of this first subdivision of the main theme.

Coupled with illustrations of the prodigal corruptions of the courts are numerous statements regarding the scramble for courtly reward. Flamineo describes his youth in terms of such activity. It is a degrading experience, dangerous and dishonorable.

> Remember this you slave, when knaves come to preferment
> they rise as gallowses are raised i'th' low countries,
> one upon another's shoulders.
> (II, i, 316)

Throughout the play, Flamineo is interested only in obtaining preferment, even if he must prostitute his sister. He is a professional at the game of courtly reward. There is no suggestion of affection for Brachiano, or even of loyalty. Everything he does for the Duke is motivated by cynical self-interest. He recognizes his activity as being essentially predatory, but, more important to him, insecure and unprofitable. Nevertheless, he has no alternate way of life, and if he had, it is doubtful that he would choose it. The struggle for courtly reward is too thoroughly ingrained in him as a way of life to allow him to change.

In his quarrel with Marcello preceding the arraignment scene, Flamineo states fully his thought on the subject. When Marcello accuses his brother of procuring their sister for Brachiano, Flamineo replies that it has been to the interests both of himself and of Vittoria to serve Brachiano, and adds,

> thou art a soldier,
> Followest the great Duke, feedest his victories,
> As witches do their serviceable spirits,
> Even with thy prodigal blood—what hast got
> But like the wealth of Captains, a poor handful?—
> Which in thy palm thou bear'st, as men hold water—
> Seeking to grip it fast, the frail reward
> Steals through thy fingers. . . .
> Thou hast scarce maintenance
> To keep thee in fresh shamois. . . .
> And thus when we have even poured our selves,
> Into great fights, for their ambition
> Or idle spleen, how shall we find reward? . . .
> Alas the poorest of their forc'd dislikes
> At a limb proffers, but at heart it strikes:
> This is lamented doctrine.
>   (III, i, 38, 57)

What Flamineo means is that any service rendered to a prince is folly. All a courtier can hope is that if he bends pliantly to the whims of his lord, he may be thrown scraps. There is no distinction, in Flamineo's mind, between Marcello's honest soldiering and his own dishonest route to preferment. The results for both will be poverty and perhaps such punishment as Lodovico has earlier received for similar services.

It is important that Flamineo have no illusions about courtly reward. He predicts his own failure, yet still hopes to avoid it. In the end, when hope is gone, he becomes a powerful example

of the folly of pursuing preferment. All that he prophesies comes
ironically true. Courtly reward has played him false. The man
who knows the game is cast down from his prince to his death.
When even the professional cannot succeed, what remains to be
said for such a way of life, other than that it is dangerous folly?

The third aspect of the central theme, the cruelty, treachery,
and injustice of a prince's vengeance, is exemplified by the behavior of Brachiano and of Francisco and Monticelso. Brachiano poisons his wife. Francisco and Monticelso indicate their
willingness to ruin Vittoria and her lover even at the cost of
Camillo's life. These princes will stop at nothing. Their ruthlessness is made clear in Act IV, scene i, where much of the dialogue is given to thematic statement. Here Francisco is shown
putting off Monticelso's incitement to revenge by a pious dissertation on the evils of starting a war against Brachiano. Monticelso, however, counsels treachery, not open warfare.

> Bear your wrongs conceal'd,
> And, patient as the Tortoise, let this Camel
> Stalk o'er your back unbruis'd: sleep with the Lion,
> And let this brood of secure foolish mice
> Play with your nostrils, till the time be ripe
> For th' bloody audit, and the fatal gripe:
> Aim like a cunning fowler, close one eye,
> That you the better may your game espy.
>
> (IV, i, 16)

This is an explicit statement of the manner in which princes work
their punishments. Although Francisco appears to disclaim such
methods, when Monticelso leaves the stage momentarily the
Duke informs the audience that he is plotting just such treachery.
He feels, however, that Monticelso is not to be trusted and states
that he prefers to work alone. Princely treachery is thus translated from precept into dog-eat-dog action.

During the fifth act the theme is fully developed, and its three divisions are woven inextricably into the action. The marriage of Brachiano and Vittoria seems to Flamineo an assurance that at last he will gain preferment.

> In all the weary minutes of my life,
> Day ne'er broke up till now. This marriage
> Confirms me happy.
>
> (V, i, 1)

Life for the first time is promising, and Flamineo's prospects belie his prophecies, but, in the ironic scene that follows, Brachiano enters and with splendid munificence assigns the Moor, Mulinassar, a "competent pension" in return for his proffered services. It is a clear example of the courtly reward which Flamineo has sought, but neither he nor Brachiano knows that Mulinassar is Francisco, disguised in pursuit of his treacherous revenge. Francisco is a realization, in dramatic terms, of the concept of princely vengeance. As an instrument of courtly punishment, Francisco is presented with a courtly reward. The two concepts merge, and from the resultant irony arises the foreshadowing of disaster to the good fortune which Flamineo thought to have.

Francisco joins his henchmen Lodovico and Gasparo to discuss the possible ways of murdering Brachiano. Lodovico takes an inhuman relish in plotting the crime so that it will stand out as a work of art in an age of diabolical killings. But Francisco puts an end to such virtuosity by demanding the quickest and surest way. This development of the cruelty of courtly punishment is interrupted by Flamineo, who warns Francisco of the fickleness of princes and the capriciousness of their promises. He tells Francisc. to get the promised reward in his hands before he counts on it. Even with fair prospects before him, Flamineo has no trust in the liberality of princes.

The evil life of the courts is exhibited in the sequence. Mar-

cello becomes enraged at Zanche's boast that she will marry
Flamineo. When Flamineo elects to defend her, the brothers
quarrel, and Marcello sends his sword to Flamineo as a challenge. Flamineo returns the sword by stabbing it in Marcello's
back, and Marcello dies, attributing his death to Vittoria's attempt
"to rise by all dishonest means." Yet to come is an exemplifica-
tion of this truth and of other warnings inherent in the theme.

Flamineo sees his prospects ruined. Brachiano punishes him
cruelly for Marcello's death by forcing him to sue for renewed
pardon each day of his life. This capricious punishment is meted
out because Flamineo once dared to "brave" him in the House
of Convertites. Flamineo now realizes that all hope for courtly
reward is gone. Neither he nor Brachiano realizes, however, that
even as the one sentences the other, courtly punishment and
courtly vengeance are again being exemplified, for, at the rear
of the stage, Lodovico is sprinkling Brachiano's helmet with
poison. When the great Duke is next seen, he is shrieking for
an armorer to tear off the burning mask. In his fury he con-
demns the armorer to torture; without hope of recovery, he can
only wait for death.

At this point, Webster introduces a new element in the theme
which links with the conception of the fickleness of court sycophants: the horror and loneliness that surround the deaths of
princes. Brachiano's torment is set off against Flamineo's unfeel-
ing commentary on the "solitariness . . . about dying Princes."
But Webster relied on more forceful means than choral comment
to dramatize his theme. A few moments later, Brachiano is
brought in on his deathbed. Alone with him, Lodovico and Gasparo torment him with his sins and strangle him. His dying cry,
"Vittoria! Vittoria!"—in itself an ironic comment on his defeat
—calls his court about him. Vittoria, when she realizes he is
dead, rushes from the unbearable room. The others murmur,
"Rest to his soul," and at this point Flamineo resumes his com-

mentary. Francisco observes with a note of wonder that Vittoria takes Brachiano's death so heavily. Flamineo shrugs:

> O yes, yes;
> Had women navigable rivers in their eyes
> They would dispend them all; . . . I'll tell thee,
> These are but Moonish shades of griefs or fears,
> There's nothing sooner dry than women's tears.
> Why here's an end of all my harvest, he has given me
>   nothing.
> Court promises! Let wisemen count them curst,
> For while you live he that scores best pays worst.
>   (V, iii, 183, 192)

He continues in the same vein, repeating much that he has previously said about the solitary deaths of princes, and exemplifying his statement by his conduct. As he leaves the stage, Zanche, Vittoria's Moorish maid, enters. The maid has become enamored of Francisco in his Moor's disguise, and, by way of courtship, exchanges lewd "dreams" with her prospective lover:

> *Zanche:* Methought sir, you came stealing to my bed.
> *Francisco:* Wilt thou believe me sweeting?—by this light
>   I was a-dreamt on thee too: for methought
>   I saw thee naked. . . .
>   And lest thou shouldst take cold, I cover'd thee
>   With this Irish mantle.
> *Zanche:*   Verily I did dream,
>   You were somewhat bold with me; but to come to't—
> *Lodovico:* How? How? I hope you will not go to it here. . . .
> *Francisco:* When I threw the mantle o'er thee, thou didst
>   laugh
>   Exceedingly methought. . . . And cried'st out,
>   The hair did tickle thee. . . .
> *Lodovico:* Mark her I prithee, she simpers like the suds
>   A Collier hath been wash'd in.
>   (V, iii, 232, 249)

Lodovico has told Brachiano that he will be forgotten before his
funeral sermon, and Zanche and Francisco provide the living
proof. For, as they speak, Brachiano's body lies on the bed in
full view of the audience! Webster says much about the solitary
deaths of princes, but nowhere does he dramatize it so effectively
as by juxtaposing Brachiano's death with the scene between these
"lovers." The great Duke dies, not in glory, not even in peace,
but in torment. Any residual illusion of greatness about his death
is dispersed by the callous scene between his murderer and the
Duchess' servant.

Brachiano's death leaves Flamineo still some hope for preferment. The Duke has settled his estate upon Vittoria until his son
Giovanni comes of age. Flamineo's first move is to court the boy.
Giovanni, however, will have nothing to do with him and forbids
him the court. In a last effort, Flamineo goes to test Vittoria's
bounty and to "sum up all these horrors." Vittoria gives him
nothing for his services but Cain's portion—"A most courtly
Patent to beg by." He tests her once more by the mock death and
only proves her ingratitude further. All he can do now is to kill
her. But he is interrupted by Lodovico and Gasparo, who inflict
the last of Francisco's courtly punishments. The brother and
sister die, and their murderer is led away to torture, exulting in
their deaths. As he goes, the audience is permitted to shudder
once more at the terrible fanaticism of courtly punishment. Lodovico says,

> I do glory yet,
> That I can call this act mine own: For my part,
> The rack, the gallows, and the torturing wheel
> Shall be but sound sleeps to me, here's my rest—
> "I limn'd this night-piece and it was my best.
>   (V, vi, 295)

The spectacle of courtly reward and punishment has run its
course; the horrors are summed up; the courtly way of life is

seen without illusion. And, though Lodovico's words are the final statement of any single aspect of the theme, all themes find their summation in the couplet Vittoria speaks as she dies:

> O happy they that never saw the Court,
> "Nor ever knew great Man but by report.
>
> (V, vi, 261)

Satire, if it is not completely irresponsible, while it traffics heavily in exaggeration, presumably retains a serious ethical purpose. In Webster's time, satire was intended to "Learn out Virtue by her contraries," to cast opprobrium on moral abuses, so that the flaying exposure might lead to moral regeneration. In the Elizabethan formal verse satires, such a purpose was the only possible justification for the enormities of the subject matter. Similarly, reform was the goal of the action of most satiric drama. In Jonson's satiric plays, for instance, the exemplary fools are brought by the machinations of the wit-intriguers to a realization of their folly, and so to a reformed life. And, in less clearly satiric drama, such as *The Honest Whore,* satire serves the uses of the reformers when Hippolito subjects Bellafront to a scathing exposure of her vices, with the result that she completely changes her way of life.

In Websterian tragedy, the efficacy of the satire in promoting reform is not so clear. Inasmuch as *The White Devil* makes use of the themes and techniques of Elizabethan satire, it might reasonably be expected that the satirist's ultimate moral advice would be found in the positive realization to which a character comes as he reviews the course of his life. Vittoria's final couplet speaks for them all. Yet, translated into positive action, it can mean but one thing: in Antonio's dying words, to "fly the Courts of Princes." No other positive, reformatory action is possible in

the light of the thematic content of the play. But whether this
advice was to be taken seriously is uncertain. Nowhere in *The
White Devil* does Webster present anyone who would or could
shun the court and the prospect of courtly reward. It is truly a
"god that governs the whole world."

Those who are not vicious are as hopelessly embroiled in the
meshes of court life as are the men and women with an evil
streak. Cornelia and Isabella meet tragedy despite their virtue,
and Marcello, though he talks of moral integrity, is dependent
on courtly reward for his living. At what is possibly a better
opportunity, he leaves Flamineo's service and comes to Brachiano's, but there is no nobler way of life for him in such a world.
Vittoria and Flamineo certainly would not have shunned the
courts of princes. Vittoria's ambition for power and wealth made
her a part of court society. Flamineo is left with no other prospect than to glean reward through courtly service. His hopes,
like those of Vittoria, are high, and, despite dishonor, he will
not give over his way of life. Any thought of avoiding the court
would be, in either of them, empty idealism. They would have
fled as far from court, perhaps, as the Petit Trianon is from the
Palace at Versailles. At most they would have sought out for an
afternoon a summerhouse, "Down by the river Tiber."

By presenting his counsel through characters whose lives demonstrate that they cannot follow such counsel, Webster implicitly
denied the possibility of action in accordance with the precepts
of his satire. He suggested that for the men and women of this
world there was no escape from evil. Economically they were
dependent on it; in their ambitions and their lusts they sought it;
their virtues were destroyed by it. They were shackled so tightly
that flight was impossible. And Webster was soon to show that
if they tried to escape, as the Duchess of Malfi did, renouncing
titles and wealth, evil followed them still, along the open country
roads.

It is not, however, only a kind of economic determinism that negates the positive aspects of the satirical counsel. In spite of his characters' failure to act on their own advice, Webster uses satire in the spirit of the sternest moralist, to emphasize the ugly realities of life. It might be argued, therefore, that even if Vittoria and Flamineo do not heed the counsel, others—those in the audience—might be led to a better life through dread of the example set before them. But even this corrective intention is vitiated when Webster suggests that the satirical utterances are motivated not by reformative zeal but by degenerate, venal policy. In Websterian tragedy, the corrective purposes of formal verse satire are nullified because satire is given most frequently to the Machiavels as a means of attacking their enemies.

Monticelso's "Character of a Whore" provides clear evidence of this negation of satire. There is nothing novel in the terms Monticelso uses to paint Vittoria's character in the arraignment scene. The images of counterfeit coins, of adulterate deceitful things, were the stock in trade of earlier satirists. Edward Gilpin's second satire in *Skialethia* closely parallels Monticelso's description, and both have a tone of rigorous moral loathing for such women. It is, of course, perfectly in character for Monticelso to make such an accusation. He is a cardinal, and soon becomes Pope. Furthermore, since Vittoria has sinned, satire of this sort is his right. Yet Monticelso's motives are not so free from suspicion as Gilpin's. Webster makes it apparent that throughout the trial Monticelso is using the machinery of the law to effect his private revenge against a woman not wholly evil. All morality is subverted to the personal ends of a venal, unscrupulous man. "Sometimes," as Bosola says, "the Devil doth preach," and when he does, firm moral ground trembles and moral footholds give way. In Webster's use of satire an instrument of morality becomes an instrument of vice, with the result that evil appears to absorb the good. Its omnipotence perverts all positive ethical counsel. Its omnipresence makes it impossible for positive moral action to arise. When it is controlled by the malevolent, morality itself is only appearance.

Despite the quantity of positive ethical statement in *The White Devil,* the final impression which the play leaves is that evil is so pervasive as to nullify any absolute, positive counsel. What to earlier satirists had been aberrations from a norm of good become not aberrations but reality. Evil is normal and nothing is to be found which will change this condition, for Webster's art proved truer than his superficial ethic, and he refused to shape his tragedy to conform with easy moralizing. Yet, however courageous a writer may be, he cannot maintain such a view of the world for long without attacking what he sees or at the very least exploring more thoroughly the nature of the evil, trying to understand its form and character in relation to its origins and ends. Lacking the only weapon for a direct attack on evil, a positive ethic, Webster chose the alternative and looked again, more deeply, at a world throttled by evil.

"A Perspective that shows us hell"

In *The Duchess of Malfi* the themes of the corruption of court life and of courtly reward and punishment are continued. Antonio's description of the ideal French court with which the play opens and his dying request, "And let my Son, fly the Courts of Princes," are sufficient evidence that the themes of *The White Devil* are present in the later play. But in the second tragedy they are no longer central. *The White Devil* is intensely concerned with the Jacobean world, treating the evils which man creates—the forces of social tyranny. The drama only hints at forces more profound than those created by man, as in the overtones of such a line as Brachiano's:

On pain of death, let no man name death to me,

> It is a word infinitely terrible—
>
> (V, iii, 39)

There is a suggestion here of something deeper, working in
secret to produce a greater horror than man can bring on himself—a natural evil which man cannot control.

The Duchess of Malfi turns the few dark hints of the sister
tragedy into actuality. It brings into focus on the stage all the
terrors of a dying universe. Not sudden death, but dying by slow
degrees, sinking into a morass of disease and rot—this is what
the human integrity must now face. The theme of social evil,
which in the earlier play is called courtly reward and punishment, is still heard, but now it is only a part of a much greater
whole, as when an actor playing a scene before the curtain is
suddenly refocused into a much larger world of activity by the
drawing of the curtain to reveal the entire stage.

As in *The White Devil,* the theme is stated early in the play.
At the beginning of the second act, Bosola mocks the gull Castruchio and the old woman who, presumably, is midwife to the
Duchess. In words reminiscent of the "comical satire" plays,
Bosola demonstrates how Castruchio can be taken for an eminent courtier. He then turns on the crone and mocks her for
painting her face, as the formal verse satirists flayed their subjects for the same offense. Antonio has called Bosola a malcontent and a victim of a foul melancholy; and it seems, as Bosola
speaks, as if the black bile rises high in his gorge, forcing him
to move from disgust at the specimens before him to a general
loathing of all humankind.

Having finished with Castruchio, Bosola proceeds to an analysis of the midwife's closet.

> One would suspect it for a shop of witch-craft, to find
> in it the fat of Serpents; spawn of Snakes, Jews' spittle,
> and their young children's ordures—and all these for
> the face: I would sooner eat a dead pigeon, taken from

the soles of the feet of one sick of the plague, than kiss
one of you fasting: here are two of you, whose sin of
your youth is the very patrimony of the Physician,
makes him renew his foot-cloth with the Spring, and
change his high-pric'd courtezan with the fall of the
leaf: I do wonder you do not loathe your selves—
observe my meditation now:

(II, i, 37)

Bosola suddenly forgets his victim and turns savagely on mankind. Webster indicates the significance of the passage with the
verbal colon, "observe my meditation now," and a change from
prose to verse.

>   observe my meditation now:
> What thing is in this outward form of man
> To be belov'd? we account it ominous,
> If Nature do produce a Colt, or Lamb,
> A Fawn, or Goat, in any limb resembling
> A Man; and fly from't as a prodigy.
> Man stands amaz'd to see his deformity,
> In any other Creature but himself.
> But in our own flesh, though we bear diseases
> Which have their true names only ta'en from beasts,
> As the most ulcerous Wolf, and swinish Measle;
> Though we are eaten up of lice, and worms,
> And though continually we bear about us
> A rotten and dead body, we delight
> To hide it in rich tissue—all our fear,
> (Nay all our terror) is, lest our Physician
> Should put us in the ground, to be made sweet.

(II, i, 45)

The speech confronts the audience with the loathsome reality of
the processes of natural decay, a subject which was barely suggested amid the social evils of *The White Devil.* In *The Duchess
of Malfi,* the theme of natural evil is central to the play.

This theme, like that of courtly reward and punishment, is

divided into three parts which are treated concurrently through the tragedy: first, the bestiality of man; second, the conception of the rotting body, accompanied by images of sexuality and of widespread corruption; and third, the dignity of death.

The first two aspects of the theme are, like the theme of courtly reward and punishment in the sister tragedy, satiric common-places, and Webster's initial treatment of the conventional material is in the tradition of formal satire. His verse is vivid and, in the passages leading to Bosola's meditation, Webster is content to let the themes reside in the images of the dialogue. Comparisons of men with animals, insects, and rapacious birds fill the first act.

> He, and his brother, are like Plum-trees (that grow crooked over standing-pools) they are rich, and o'er-laden with Fruit, but none but Crows, Pies, and Cater-pillars feed on them: Could I be one of their flattering Panders, I would hang on their ears like a horse-leech, till I were full, and then drop off.
>
> (I, i, 50)

> The Spring in his face, is nothing but the Engend'ring of Toads.
>
> (I, i, 159)

> . . . the Law to him
> Is like a foul black cob-web, to a Spider—
> He makes it his dwelling, and a prison
> To entangle those shall feed him.
>
> (I, i, 180)

The second thematic element is presented in similar fashion. The degeneration of the body, sexuality, and less specific personal or social corruption provide images which establish at the outset the play's basic concerns.

> If too immoderate sleep be truly said
> To be an inward rust unto the soul;

It then doth follow want of action
Breeds all black malcontents, and their close rearing
(Like moths in cloth) do hurt for want of wearing.

(I, i, 79)

There's no more credit to be given to th' face,
Than to a sick man's urine, which some call
The Physician's whore, because she cozens him.

(I, i, 250)

Ferdinand: A Vizor, and a Mask are whispering rooms
　　That were nev'r built for goodness: fare ye well:
　　And women like that part, which (like the Lamprey)
　　Hath nev'r a bone in't.

Duchess: Fie Sir!

Ferdinand: Nay,
　　I mean the Tongue: variety of Courtship . . .

(I, i, 373)

what's my place?

The Provisor-ship o'th' horse? say then my corruption
Grew out of horse-dung.

(I, i, 311)

a Prince's Court

Is like a common Fountain, whence should flow
Pure silver-drops in general: But if't chance
Some curs'd example poison't near the head,
"Death, and diseases through the whole land spread.

(I, i, 12)

Bosola's "meditation" synthesizes and makes explicit the first
two elements of the main theme; thereafter the animal metaphor
and the images of degeneration flood the dialogue. The pregnancy of the Duchess is described in terms of the corruption of
the flesh. Later, Bosola again waylays the midwife, and jibes
at her with allusions to sexual abnormality. During the confusion
attendant upon the birth of the child, the servants spread lewd
tales of a Switzer caught in the Duchess' bedroom with a pistol

in his codpiece. Soon thereafter, Ferdinand and the Cardinal swear vengeance on their sister. Their words, filled with images of bestiality and degeneration, are like a summary of what has gone before.

> *Ferdinand:* Methinks I see her laughing,
> Excellent *Hyena*—talk to me somewhat, quickly,
> Or my imagination will carry me
> To see her, in the shameful act of sin.
> *Cardinal:* With whom?
> *Ferdinand:* Happily, with some strong-thigh'd Bargeman;
> Or one o'th' wood-yard, that can quoit the sledge,
> Or toss the bar, or else some lovely Squire
> That carries coals up, to her privy lodgings. . . .
> Go to (Mistress)
> 'Tis not your whore's milk, that shall quench my wild-fire,
> But your whore's blood.
> *Cardinal:* How idly shows this rage! . . . I can be angry
> Without this rupture—there is not in nature
> A thing, that makes man so deform'd, so beastly,
> As doth intemperate anger.

(II, v, 52, 76)

Throughout the first part of the play Webster never ceases to emphasize these thematic metaphors, which stress vividly man's bestiality and degeneration by frank statement and vile suggestion.

But such evil was to become more than a metaphor. What to the satirists had been commonplace comparisons are turned unexpectedly into living reality, when at the end of the play the animal image is translated into action in Ferdinand's madness. Ferdinand falls victim to lycanthropy, the "melancholy humour" whereby men imagine themselves to be transformed into wolves,

> Steal forth to Church-yards in the dead of night,
> And dig dead bodies up.

(V, ii, 12)

The incident was carefully planned. Ferdinand's mind, long
before he becomes irrational, is dwelling on wolves. He com-
pares the Duchess' voice to the howling of a wolf. Her children
are "Cubs," and he says, when he views their bodies,

> The death
> Of young Wolves, is never to be pitied.
> (IV, ii, 274)

When Ferdinand goes mad, the image becomes actuality. The
beast in man appears in its grimmest, most horrible manifestation. Ferdinand *is* an animal. The metaphor is interpreted lit-
erally, and presented in a way unknown to the formal satirists,
as reality that underlay the cause of evil in the outward form of
man. Bosola had said, "Man stands amaz'd to see his deformity, /
In any other Creature but himself," and Webster expected his
audience to stand amazed at this spectacle of the bestial over-
throwing the human. With the animal metaphor he deliberately
set the deformities of men, physical and spiritual, into relief
against a world of unregulated instincts.

Images of sex, general corruption, and bodily rot, like the animal images, appeared frequently in the work of other satirists.
Marston and Tourneur are full of them. Again, however, Webster did not stop with the images, but showed them in action.
The scene in which Julia, the Cardinal's depraved mistress, woos
Bosola to her bed is sufficient example of the realization of
sexual images in the dramatic action. Its surface is strangely
quiet, almost casually straightforward. But the strength and the
ugliness of the episode come from its startling echo of the scene
in which the Duchess proposes to Antonio. The Duchess had said,

> The misery of us, that are born great!—
> We are forc'd to woo, because none dare woo us: . . .
> I do here put off all vain ceremony,
> And only do appear to you a young widow

> That claims you for her husband, and like a widow,
> I use but half a blush in't.
> (I, i, 507, 525)

In similar words, Julia cajoles the man she wants:

> Now you'll say,
> I am wanton: This nice modesty, in Ladies
> Is but a troublesome familiar,
> That haunts them. . . . I am sudden with you—
> We that are great women of pleasure, use to cut off
> These uncertain wishes, and unquiet longings,
> And in an instant join the sweet delight
> And the pretty excuse together.
> (V, ii, 176, 205)

Although the scenes are placed at opposite ends of the play, the similarity is striking. Certainly, in contrast with the beauty and health of the earlier scene, the later parallel becomes an active manifestation of the images of sexual corruption which infest the drama.

In like manner, the images of widespread social and individual corruption become more than metaphors. As in *The White Devil,* the behavior of the great princes and prelates is thoroughly dishonest. The machinations of Ferdinand and the Cardinal, the Cardinal's stealthy attempts to cover his part in the crime, the spectacle of sycophants, flatterers, intelligencers, and murderers which surround the Aragonian brothers make the images of social corruption appallingly real. As for the moral corruption of the individual, there is Bosola, whose life is a voluntary embracing of such evil.

With the images pertaining to bodily rot, Webster approaches the farthest reaches of terror. Bosola had lamented that "though continually we bear about us / A rotten and dead body, we delight / To hide it in rich tissue." In the fourth act, this aspect of the central theme is used to rouse the Duchess to the fullest assertion of her integrity. The body, he tells her, is rotten, weak, worthless.

> Thou art a box of worm-seed, at best, but a salvatory
> of green mummy: what's this flesh? a little crudded
> milk, fantastical puff-paste: our bodies are weaker
> than those paper prisons boys use to keep flies in: more
> contemptible: since ours is to preserve earth-worms.
>
> (IV, ii, 123)

It is the ultimate degradation, the final revelation of the reality beneath the Duchess' dignified and gracious appearance. But it is this image which enables her to assert, in spite of the worthlessness of her outward form, that she is "Duchess of *Malfi* still."

In the development of the third thematic division, the dignity of death, Webster sounded the depths of the problem of evil which he had first faced in *The White Devil*. Bosola's "meditation" gives the theme preliminary statement.

> all our fear,
> (Nay all our terror) is, lest our Physician
> Should put us in the ground, to be made sweet.

Images of death are everywhere in *The Duchess of Malfi*. They all but dominate the proposal scene. Ferdinand conjures up fantastic ways of murdering the Duchess and her husband, and his images of murder twine with the sexual imagery to create a horrifying effect.

> I would have their bodies
> Burnt in a coal-pit, with the ventage stopp'd,
> That their curs'd smoke might not ascend to Heaven:
> Or dip the sheets they lie in, in pitch or sulphur,
> Wrap them in't, and then light them like a match:
> Or else to boil their Bastard to a cullis,
> And give't his lecherous father, to renew
> The sin of his back.
>
> (II, v, 87)

There are the strange, hysterical images of death the Duchess evoked when she was confronted by the strangling cord. There is Bosola, disguised as a maker of tombs; there are the wax figures and the dead man's hand; and there are the murders of the Duchess and the screaming Cariola. In almost every scene, death makes its appearance.

The fifth act has repeatedly been criticized as an anticlimactic cluttering of the stage with corpses. It is true that with the death of the Duchess in the fourth act a light goes out of the play. The heroic story has been told. But the satiric story, the revelation of the real condition of man's world, has not been completed. The fifth act with its frightening development of the theme of death is essential to the picture of the tragic world.

The fourth act shows the destruction of good by evil and the way in which humanity can assert its integrity even in defeat. The fifth act shows what happens in a world where good is dead and integrity is absent. The lascivious Julia is murdered by her lover. Antonio is killed in error by the man who sought to save him. The Cardinal is trapped by Bosola. A servant who attempts to summon help is stabbed. The Cardinal's screams for help rouse the lunatic Ferdinand, and in the three-way scuffle the "wretched eminent things" are fatally wounded. Evil turns on evil: these are the rampaging disasters that follow the destruction of good, the full flood tide of death. The last act of the tragedy does indeed present what William Archer called a "butcher's bill"; but it is not without meaning.

The deaths in *The Duchess of Malfi* are different in their effect from the slaughters in *The White Devil.* In the latter, the murders were the working out of social evils, the product of deliberate vengeance. Francisco and Monticelso are alive at the play's end, triumphant in what they have done. With the exception of Flamineo, the characters are in no sense resigned to their deaths. In *The Duchess of Malfi,* however, Webster is careful to show

that all the important characters except the hysterical Cariola
and the insane Ferdinand welcome death as inevitable. They
seem to feel that death is not the result of man's inhumanity to
man so much as a slight hastening of the processes of natural
decay and a return, ultimately, to sweetness. The Cardinal asks
"to be laid by, and never thought of." Bosola's soul is weary.
Antonio senses that life is merely "a preparative to rest." Their
words echo those of the Duchess:

> Tell my brothers,
> That I perceive death, (now I am well awake)
> Best gift is, they can give, or I can take— . . .
> Come violent death,
> Serve for *Mandragora,* to make me sleep.
>   (IV, ii, 229, 242)

There is terror in this death struggle of evil, but there is dignity
as well, and quiet—a quiet that seems almost an answer to the
tormenting problems of the world.

Death and the Dignity of Man

The White Devil is a tragedy of disillusion, *The Duchess of Malfi,*
a tragedy of despair. The first is concerned with worldly corruption, but in Vittoria, Brachiano, Flamineo, Francisco, and the
Cardinal there is shown to be a quality of grandeur, a faint
tracing of an idealistic conception of mankind. These people
retain a suggestion of greatness, but the satire shows that it lies
not in power or rank, but in individualism which cannot be
destroyed. The greatness is often adulterated with evil, yet it is
evil that seems to exist on a mundane level, with its cause in
the actions of men. If men cause it, men presumably can control it, and throughout the play there are hints at this possibility.
    In *The Duchess of Malfi,* however, the controls are no longer

in the hands of man. Social corruption is but one manifestation of a decaying world. Decay is everywhere. It is in the body, which is "to preserve earth-worms." It breaks through the bars of the mind to let the beast in man roam loose. It confounds even good deeds with tragic error. The pathway to death is the gutter, the sewer, the dung heap. In the end, man is powerless to foster good or to check evil, because death surrounds all actions and renders them meaningless. Both good and evil are appearances when seen against the background of common mortality. Such a view of the world, more profound than one of disillusion, leads to despair.

Death in Websterian tragedy is a word "infinitely terrible," but it is in no way so terrible a word as life. By comparison, death and oblivion are infinitely welcome. Brachiano had found it a miserable thing to die "'Mongst women howling." The fear of oblivion rises high in the great duke as Lodovico and Gasparo taunt him with mortality. He, however, is the only one of the characters who dies in misery, except for the "womanish and fearful" Cariola. Brachiano, like Cariola, is prepared for death neither by his integrity of spirit nor by his weariness of the world. On the other characters, a blessed anonymity descends as they go to their graves. Whereas Hamlet died begging Horatio to clear his name to the world, Webster's men and women crave and receive oblivion. The Cardinal asks to be forgotten, Ferdinand "vaults" the credit of the world, and Antonio does not want the story of his death to be told. Bosola, as he dies, says,

> We are only like dead walls, or vaulted graves,
> That ruin'd, yields no echo.
>
> (V, v, 121)

In *The White Devil,* though they face death courageously, the characters seem unaware of its deeper significance. They are not weary enough of life to leave it gladly. The only exception

is Flamineo, who, strangely enough, says the word for the men
and women of the later tragedy:

> "We cease to grieve, cease to be fortune's slaves,
> "Nay cease to die by dying.
>
> (V, vi, 252)

And a moment later,

> "This busy trade of life appears most vain,
> "Since rest breeds rest, where all seek pain by pain.
>
> (V, vi, 273)

In *The White Devil,* Flamineo alone recognized this. In *The
Duchess of Malfi* it becomes the common chord of resolution.

It is strange that in these plays so little is made of the hope
for an afterlife. The ghosts prove nothing in regard to Webster's
conception. Of the two in *The White Devil,* Brachiano's is an
omen, like the echo from the Duchess' tomb, to predict approach-
ing death; and Isabella's apparition is felt by Francisco to be in
his mind and not a supernatural manifestation. There are no
ghosts in *The Duchess of Malfi;* in that play, the undiscovered
country lies "in a mist."

The characters themselves, except for the Duchess, do not
express much hope of a heaven. The Duchess dies confident that
she will be reunited with Antonio, but this seems more a part of
her character than evidence of Webster's conviction. Vittoria
seems to make a phrase of the concept when she demands that
Lodovico kill her before he murders her maid.

> You shall not kill her first. Behold my breast,
> I will be waited on in death; my servant
> Shall never go before me.
>
> (V, vi, 217)

Judging from the absence of this idea where it was most needed
to convert despair to hope, it would seem that Webster was

unable to lift his eyes from the grave to the hills. He speaks, perhaps, in Flamineo's words:

"While we look up to heaven we confound
"Knowledge with knowledge. ô I am in a mist.
                    (V, vi, 259)

The knowledge of heaven is confounded by the knowledge of earth, as the good on earth is absorbed and confounded by evil. In the darkness there is no clue to the light.

If there was no concept of heaven, there was little thought of suicide, stoic or other. When Flamineo, at the end of *The White Devil,* says that he is going to kill himself "With as much pleasure / As e'er my father gat me," Vittoria replies,

Are you grown an Atheist? will you turn your body,
Which is the goodly palace of the soul
To the soul's slaughter house?
                    (V, vi, 57)

But Flamineo's suicidal intentions are a part of his plot to kill his sister, and Vittoria is talking to gain time. Both remarks arise from the exigencies of the situation. Again, the Duchess in hysteria talks of suicide. Bosola warns her against despair, and she replies,

              The Church enjoins fasting:
I'll starve my self to death.
                    (IV, i, 89)

This, however, is close to madness and is shortly forgotten.

In Websterian tragedy, life is a horror, and death, though terrible, is to be desired. Yet an escape from life is not to be sought in death. The solution to this paradox lies in struggling while life lasts to preserve integrity. To do so is not easy. Evil is no passive or neutral condition; it is an active force, welling up through the natural world in disease and madness, and through human society in vicious action. But the hero will not fly to his death as the Duchess would at first have fled to Ancona. He will approach it, as Bosola counseled the Duchess to follow Antonio, making a "Princely progress," meeting it, as Vittoria met her death, in the manner of a Prince greeting "some great Ambassadors." Stoical resistance, though it provides no remedy, at least asserts the dignity of man. Such assertion is the proof of integrity of life, and in the world where good is alien, integrity is the only real value.

Integrity of life carries its own protection in its self-sufficiency. It flourishes in adversity; in the lowest depths it achieves the sublime. After evil has done its worst to the Duchess, she finds the courage to assert the "spirit of greatness." In witnessing such assertion, the audience discovers that death, to which evil has brought her, is her greatest triumph. She has made the "Princely progress" through evil, not to good, but to the assertion of the single value in life that can be maintained while life lasts.

Only Vittoria and Flamineo, among the other characters in Websterian tragedy, find the courage to make this assertion. If their deaths seem less moving, it is perhaps because Webster did not quite realize the significance of their action. He had not yet fully explored the depths of the tragic world. Nevertheless, his instinct was true, and they, like the Duchess of Malfi, achieve greatness at the end. For the others there seems to be a partial value in dying well, especially if one dies as Bosola does, in a good cause. The ability to meet death without whining has some of the courage of assertion. But there is no greatness in it, for integrity of life is not a way of dying. As the Duchess, Vittoria, and Flamineo reveal, it is a way of life.

CONCLUSION:
TRAGIC SATIRE

AS WEBSTER DARKENS THE WORLD of his tragedy, life appears to become an increasing agony. What had been aberration to the earlier satirists becomes to Webster the norm. Each evil is a symbol of death, each abuse a step toward it. In the end, what his satire revealed of the true nature of life is fused with the outcome of his tragic story. The ultimate tragedy of Webster's world is not the death of any individual but the presence of evil and decay which drags all mankind to death. The function of the satire is to reveal man's common mortality and his involvement in evil; the tragic story is the story of a few who find courage to defy such revelation. In their defiance there is a glory for mankind, and in their struggle and assertion lies the brilliance of Websterian tragedy.

Yet it is important to realize that Websterian tragedy is great because of its fusion of satire and tragedy. Had this fusion been incomplete, the effect would have been destroyed. A lack of reality or of proper heightening, a failure to integrate the satiric comment—and the accusation could justly be made that these spectacles were merely sensational shows to please the vulgar. As it is, taking the dramas in their own time, in the light of the carefully developed techniques which produced them, the accusation seems in all significant instances to lack justification. Webster has

(147)

created an integrated, important world through his tragic action
which makes his plays a profound comment on life. Second only
to Shakespeare (and, with the essential differences understood,
the Shakespeare comparison can be safely resumed), Webster
has found what William Butler Yeats named "Emotion of Multitude." Yeats wrote, "Indeed all the great Masters have understood, that there cannot be great art without the little limited
life of the fable, . . . and the rich, far-wandering, many-imaged
life of the half-seen world beyond it."[1]

Shakespeare, concentrating on character, traces the wellsprings
of his tragic hero's inner being to its deep source in common
humanity. From this root comes generality—"Emotion of Multitude"—which an audience may not always consciously understand, but to which it rarely fails to respond. Webster, forgoing
significant inner revelation, traces the outer patterns of men
struggling with one another, de-emphasizing the individual aspects of his "fable," and relating its action explicitly to the action
of men everywhere. It is when the light of satiric generality
shines across the plane of tragic action and throws that action
into relief that the immense shadows of the protagonists fall
across the face of life itself. Through the "Emotion of Multitude" thus achieved, *The White Devil* and *The Duchess of Malfi*
speak as eloquently today as in the past.

The tragedies will not appeal to all audiences. Their horror
at life, their preoccupation with death have been termed un-
healthy obsessions in times characterized by ethical steadiness
and spiritual faith. Yet many twentieth-century poets have
found Webster congenial because they saw in their world a cor-
respondence with the world depicted by the dramatist. Values
crumpled in their hands as they had for Webster and his contemporaries three centuries earlier. From the very lack of values
there sprang an affinity.

There comes a time, however, when denial of value has to

cease. Man must find, or convince himself that he can find, something in the world which is not prey to rot and human bestiality. It has proved so with the poets of the 1920's, and possibly something of the kind happened with Webster. Perhaps the lost drama *Guise,* which he mentions in the preface to *The Devil's Law-Case* in connection with the twin tragedies, might have told more of what happened to him in his search for ethical value. As it is, all that can be stated is that the fire, which struck out of his despair and forced him to set forth on the stage what he saw in the world, died suddenly. *The White Devil* and *The Duchess of Malfi* are the only plays that have the tragic sweep, the full "Emotion of Multitude." His later tragedy grows conventional, his comedy increasingly foolish. The plays after 1614 are few, and none of them attain the tragic heights. Sometime after 1635, Webster disappeared from the scene, swallowed "in a mist" as effectively as any of his characters.

In all probability, nothing more will be learned of the man than his two tragedies revealed. But that is enough by which to know him. While his despair flamed, he presented life as he saw it, and although what he saw was undoubtedly distorted in that half-light, for the short space of Webster's life it was an aspect of the truth. His view of life was one-directional, but it was profound. He looked a long way into darkness. His characters buffet their course against a black panorama, and in the end are swallowed in shadow. Only a few, before the storm of terror breaks, can find the courage to assert the essential dignity of man. But this, as it is in any degree a picture of a world men must recognize, is, despite its horror, the stuff of tragedy.

NOTES
and REFERENCES

All quotations from Webster are from *The Complete Works of John Webster,* ed. F. L. Lucas, 4 vols. (New York, Oxford University Press, 1937). The following editions of the plays of Webster's contemporaries are frequently cited: George Chapman, *Plays and Poems,* ed. Thomas Marc Parrott, 2 vols. (London, Routledge and Kegan Paul, Ltd., 1910); John Marston, *Plays,* ed. H. Harvey Wood, 3 vols. (Edinburgh, Oliver and Boyd, Ltd., 1934–1939). Quotations from Marston's satires are from *The Works of John Marston,* ed. A. H. Bullen, 3 vols. (London, 1887).

Where reference is made to the commentary by the editors, citation of the volumes is abbreviated "Lucas," and so on. All other citations refer to the individual plays by title. *The White Devil* is abbreviated as *WD*; *The Duchess of Malfi* as *DM*.

NOTES TO THE INTRODUCTION

[1] See Charles Crawford, *Collectanea,* First Series (Stratford-on-Avon, 1906), Second Series (Stratford-on-Avon, 1907); Lucas, I, 57–63, and Commentary, *passim;* Marcia Lee Anderson, "Webster's Debt to Guazzo," *Studies in Philology,* XXXVI (1939), 192–205.

[2] John Forster and George Henry Lewes, *Dramatic Essays,* ed. William Archer and Robert Lowe (London, 1896), pp. 120–121.

[3] The comparison with Shakespeare underlies many recent essays on Webster and leads their authors to what appears to be a distorted view of the subject. For instance, W. A. Edwards sees Webster's style as "literary," "urbane," "precious," in comparison with passages from *King Lear,* and he finds that Webster's characters, when set beside Shakespeare's, reveal no profound self-knowledge, to their detriment. See "John Webster," in *Determinations,* ed. F. R. Leavis (London, Chatto and Windus, 1934), pp. 175–178. Ian Jack, who feels Webster's presentation of stoic virtue to be unrealized in the action, and who therefore argues that

(151)

the moral scheme of the tragedies is a kind of afterthought, repeatedly uses Shakespearian tragedy as a touchstone, scolding Webster for ignoring the moral traditions to which Shakespeare was indebted. See "The Case of John Webster," *Scrutiny,* XVI (1949), i, 38–43. Some essential differences between Webster and Shakespeare are discussed in David Cecil's essay published in his *Poets and Story-Tellers* (London, Constable, 1949), and he makes a case for Webster which is sharply opposed to those set forth by Edwards and Jack. Yet, in spite of his sympathy for Webster, he seems to overstate the positive as they the negative. Statements such as "Always at the end of Webster's plays the Divine Law is vindicated" (p. 34) imply a parallel with Bradley's view of Shakespearian tragedy, again in a way that distorts rather than clarifies the nature of Websterian tragedy. A similar case of sympathy errant develops in Moody E. Prior's analysis of Websterian tragedy in *The Language of Tragedy* (New York, Columbia University Press, 1947), pp. 120–121. Prior's analysis of the design of the language of the tragedies is subtle and valuable, but, although he explicitly eschews the critical position which made William Archer's frenetic attacks on Webster possible, when he turns his attention to the substance of the tragedies he makes a distinction curiously like that of Archer between Webster as poet and Webster as dramatist, and with similar results: as poet, Webster is comparable to Shakespeare; as dramatist, he is merely inept.

[4]M. C. Bradbrook, *Themes and Conventions of Elizabethan Tragedy* (Cambridge, University Press, 1935); Rupert Brooke, *John Webster and the Elizabethan Drama* (London, 1916); Una Ellis-Fermor, *The Jacobean Drama* (London, Methuen, 1936); Willard Farnham, *Shakespeare's Tragic Frontier* (Berkeley and Los Angeles, University of California Press, 1950); Clifford Leech, *John Webster* (London, Hogarth Press, 1951); Theodore Spencer, *Death and Elizabethan Tragedy* (Cambridge, Mass., Harvard University Press, 1936); E. E. Stoll, *John Webster* (Cambridge, Mass., 1905); H. W. Wells, *Elizabethan and Jacobean Playwrights* (New York, Columbia University Press, 1939); G. P. V. Akrigg, "The Anatomy of Websterian Tragedy" (unpublished dissertation, University of California, Berkeley, 1944).

[5]Wells, *Elizabethan and Jacobean Playwrights,* p. 46. Quotations used by permission of Columbia University Press.

[6]*Ibid.*

[7]Lucas, I, 197, n. to l. 41.

[8]Lucas, IV, Index to Commentary, *s. v. Jonson.* See also *WD,* III, ii, 292, and *Sejanus,* IV, v, 96–98.

[9]John Marston's theatrical career ended in 1608. *The White Devil* was published in 1612. Even so, the omission of Marston's name from the list is not entirely comprehensible. Webster's debt to Marston is, however, clear, and will be discussed later (see chap. iv).

¹⁰That the tragedies of Chapman are so unlike the tragedies of Shakespeare as to seem almost of a different kind is a point that needs no laboring. The adjective "Shakespearian" when used as a standard of definition or measurement has proved as indeterminate as the other grand adjectives of English scholarship—Romantic, Classical, Medieval. Especially when used promiscuously to praise or condemn the work of other Jacobean dramatists, it has proved singularly unhelpful. The atypical nature of Shakespeare's dramaturgy is not, in its details—even as these details bear on Webster—of particular importance to the present work. Of greater positive consequence is the crucial alliance between Webster and Chapman.

NOTES TO CHAPTER ONE

¹Drawn as he was to the work of Marlowe, Chapman may have looked more than cursorily at *The Massacre at Paris.* Yet in dramatizing events of about the same time as the massacre, he avoids the sensational religious and political episodes, going so far as to treat Marlowe's archvillain, the Guise, as a sympathetic if not heroic character. It may be, as F. S. Boas suggests, that in rejecting the opportunity to stage the lurid Huguenot massacre, Chapman was merely avoiding an elaboration on what Marlowe had successfully accomplished earlier. See George Chapman, *Bussy D'Ambois and The Revenge of Bussy D'Ambois,* ed. F. S. Boas (Boston, 1905), p. xxiv. But it may also be that he sensed more in the character of the French politicians than material for a melodrama. Continually, he turns from the sensational to seek higher ethical meaning, and, in doing so, may well have felt himself to be writing more importantly, more "truly," than Marlowe had.

²Webster and Ford are credited with what probably was just such a tabloid domestic tragedy, *A Late Murder of the Son upon the Mother.*

³Parrott, I, 593.

⁴Chapman's distortion of the popular conception of the Duke of Guise is discussed by Boas, *Bussy D'Ambois . . . ,* pp. xxxix ff. See Parrott, I, 576.

⁵Again note the elimination of the specific, localizing events of the St. Bartholomew massacre.

⁶When Webster began work on *The White Devil,* probably about 1610–1611, he could have read the first quarto of *Bussy D'Ambois,* which appeared in 1607, and perhaps could have seen a production of the revised version of the play at Whitefriars in 1610. *The Revenge of Bussy D'Ambois* was written late in 1610, although it was not published until 1613. *The Conspiracy and Tragedy of Charles Duke of Byron* appeared in 1607–1608. Of the four plays of Chapman which Webster could have known when he wrote the twin tragedies, certainly the most influential is

The Revenge of Bussy D'Ambois. It is significant that, although Webster could have known it as early as 1611, its main impact is felt not on *The White Devil* but on *The Duchess of Malfi*, written about 1613–1614, when Webster could surely have seen *The Revenge* in printed form. It should be mentioned that Webster wrote a now-lost play, *Guise*, probably on the assassination of the Duke of Guise. See *The Devil's Law-Case*, "To the Right Worthy, and All-accomplished Gentleman, Sir Thomas Finch . . ." and Lucas, II, 321, n. to l. 6. Curiously, this dedication might well be a paraphrase of the first paragraph of Chapman's dedication of *The Revenge of Bussy D'Ambois*.

[7]Lucas, I, 90.

[8]Lucas, II, 9–17.

[9]Webster's most significant departure from his sources is his change in attitude toward certain of his characters. Vittoria's mother and Brachiano's Duchess are made virtuous characters, in defiance of historical evidence. This is a slight change, but the complete reversal of Painter's and Belleforest's disapproval of the Duchess of Malfi is clearly an alteration to fit an individual conception of the basic materials.

[10]Lucas, I, 91.

[11]See Lucas, I, 96, n. 1; II, 15–17.

[12]See O. J. Campbell, *Comicall Satyre and Shakespeare's Troilus and Cressida* (San Marino, Calif., Henry E. Huntington Library, 1938), pp. 20–21.

[13]G. M. Trevelyan, *England under the Stuarts*, 6th ed. (New York, 1914), p. 110.

[14]On this passage see John Russell Brown, "On the Dating of *The White Devil* and *The Duchess of Malfi*," *Philological Quarterly*, XXXI (1952), iv, 353 ff.

[15]Chapman's stoicism has been widely investigated. See especially Jean Jacquot, *George Chapman*, Annales de l'Université de Lyon (Lettres): III, 19 (Paris, 1951); John William Wieler, *George Chapman—The Effect of Stoicism upon His Tragedies* (New York, King's Crown Press, 1949); Herschel Baker, *The Dignity of Man* (Cambridge, Mass., Harvard University Press, 1947); Janet Spens, "Chapman's Ethical Thought," *Essays and Studies by Members of the English Association*, XI (1925), pp. 145–169; Roy Battenhouse, "Chapman and the Nature of Man," *English Literary History*, XII (1945), pp. 87–107.

[16]*Bussy D'Ambois*, V, iv, 147.

[17]Spens, *op. cit.*, p. 148.

[18]In this thematic particular the structure of Chapman's tragedies is not materially different from that of many of his contemporaries. Marston, Webster, Tourneur, Ford, and, to a degree, Jonson make variations on

the same plan. Even Shakespeare, who resembles Chapman least, designed his tragedies from the common pattern, using the villains to raise the problems and provide the activity of evil, and the Senecal man to provide the explanation for the problems, and to stand as the rock against which the forces of evil eventually expend themselves. The dramatists differ in their technique far more than in thematic material.

[19]Dryden, in "The Art of Poetry," *The Poetical Works of John Dryden,* ed. George R. Noyes (Boston, 1909), III, 555–557, provides corroboration for this view of Bussy as a pattern of perfection:

> Your bully poets, bully heroes write;
> Chapman in *Bussy d'Ambois* took delight,
> And thought perfection was to huff and fight.

[20]Cf. Parrott, I, 598.

[21]Until the fifth act, Clermont takes no action, and effects his revenge only when the ghost of Bussy points out that Montsurry has escaped punishment because of the corrupt laws of the realm, and that it is up to him to perfect God's justice by killing Montsurry.

[22]The physical attack on Clermont is narrated. The dueling sequence in the fifth act is continually interrupted by "virtuous digressions." The traditional first-act appearance of the ghost, inciting the revenger to action, is omitted; and when the ghost appears, in the fifth act, he is given some of the play's weightiest philosophical exposition to deliver. The only concession to spectacle, sensational or comic, is the dance of the ghosts around the body of Montsurry at the end of the play. This, as Parrott notes, probably represents the stage manager's pathetic attempt to make his mark on the most unyielding play in the history of the stage.

NOTES TO CHAPTER TWO

[1]Compare Francisco's disguise as an honest courtier and the commentary on his behavior in *WD,* V, i, 100–111.

[2]*DM,* I, i, 500.

[3]Bosola's comment on the Cardinal's dying panic has some of the quality of Chapman's interpretation of Byron's character. See *DM,* V, v, 56–58.

[4]On the relation of Vittoria and Bosola to the revenge tradition, see F. T. Bowers, *Elizabethan Revenge Tragedy* (Princeton University Press, 1940), pp. 177–183.

Thomas Overbury, *The Overburian Characters,* ed. W. J. Paylor, Percy Reprints, XIII (Oxford, Basil Blackwell, 1936), p. 92.

[6]Lucas, IV, 6 ff.

[7]"*The Duchess of Malfi,*" Wilson wrote, "was not funny. You understood what Gertrude Stein meant when she said that she had reread in

France, during the war, Shakespeare's tragedies and historical plays and had realized for the first time that human life could be like that. . . . One saw the scene of the released lunatics, in which the Duchess of Malfi is told her doom, just at the moment of the exposé of the German prison camps. The theatre was thus a little breathless, a little tense with fear and fatigue, like everything else in London." "Notes on London at the End of a War," *The New Yorker,* June 2, 1945, pp. 47–48. Quoted by permission of *The New Yorker.*

NOTES TO CHAPTER THREE

[1]Lucas, I, 193 ff.

[2]Apparently taking their cues from Lamb, Hazlitt noted in her a "sincere sense of guilt," and Swinburne referred to her as "shame-stricken." But in the arraignment scene—and elsewhere, for that matter—there is no evidence of remorse on Vittoria's part. Shame, cowardice, hypocrisy are not part of her character. She is too proud to cringe or fawn in order to be let off. She wants not pardon but legal acquittal and, above all, treatment befitting her desired title of Duchess.

There are two charges against her in the arraignment: incontinence and murder. Vittoria takes the charge of murder, of which there is no proof, as the whole charge, and demands that it be proved or that proceedings be dropped. She denies nothing except foreknowledge of Camillo's death, and this is accomplished by means of an equivocation that is not clearly denial. Cf. III, ii, 126–127. The summit of her skillful defense is a ringing cry for strict legal proof, and it is noteworthy that she admits to more sins than they have charged her with, even while defying them to trap her:

> You are deceived.
> For know that all your strict-combined heads,
> Which strike against this mine of diamonds,
> Shall prove but glassen hammers, they shall break—
> These are but feigned shadows of my evils.
> Terrify babes, my Lord, with painted devils,
> I am past such needless palsy—for your names,
> Of Whore and Murd'ress they proceed from you,
> As if a man should spit against the wind,
> The filth returns in's face.

(III, ii, 146)

Her boldness does not much resemble innocence. The strange, almost involuntary phrase, "These are but feigned shadows of my evils," wrung from her in the heat of anger, is all but an admission of guilt.

[3]Lucas, I, 98.

[4]A statement Flamineo makes to his mother provides additional sup-

port for this interpretation of Vittoria in the light of her sexual needs. He says of women generally, but with obvious reference to Vittoria and Camillo,

> Go, go,
> Complain unto my great Lord Cardinal,
> Yet may be he will justify the act.
> *Lycurgus* wondered much, men would provide
> Good stallions for their Mares, and yet would suffer
> Their fair wives to be barren.
>
> (I, ii, 333)

⁵Lucas, I, 95.

⁶The sleep of the Duchess is a pathetic motif in the tragedy. Compare I, i, 206–207; III, ii, 14–17; IV, ii, 135–140, 241–242, 247.

⁷Lodovico displays a similar curiosity at Vittoria's reaction as he prepares to stab her: "Thou dost tremble, / Me thinks fear should dissolve thee into air." *WD*, V, vi, 222.

⁸Lucas, I, 27–28.

NOTES TO CHAPTER FOUR

¹O. J. Campbell, *Comicall Satyre and Shakespeare's Troilus and Cressida* (San Marino, California, Henry E. Huntington Library, 1938), p. 30. Quotations used by permission of the Huntington Library Press.

²The history of this satire is traced in Professor Campbell's studies, to which I am extensively indebted in these pages.

³*Antonio and Mellida* and *Antonio's Revenge* were published in 1602, but written probably in 1599. See E. K. Chambers, *The Elizabethan Stage*, 4 vols. (Oxford, 1923), III, 429–430. *The Malcontent* appeared in two editions in 1604, the second with Webster's "Additions." For demonstration of textual parallels see Lucas, index to Commentary, *s.v.* Marston. Compare *The Malcontent*, IV, v, p. 197, ll. 11–23, with *DM*, IV, ii, 123 ff; *The Malcontent*, III, ii, *passim*, with *DM*, II, i, *passim*. On the subtler manifestations of the indebtedness see Ellis-Fermor, *The Jacobean Drama*, pp. 95–96.

⁴*Antonio and Mellida*, Induction, p. 8.

⁵Campbell, *op. cit.*, p. 144.

⁶Jean Anouilh, *Antigone*, adapted by Lewis Galantière (New York, Random House, 1946), p. 37.

⁷A recent, honorable failure to make such a merging is Arthur Miller's *Death of a Salesman*, where the irony implicit in the hero's death seems to destroy the sense of his final achievement of self-recognition.

⁸O. J. Campbell, *Shakespeare's Satire* (New York, Oxford University Press, 1943), p. 167. Quotation used by permission of the publisher.

The ellipsis marks the omission of the words "and futilely," which, though certainly true of such plays as *Troilus and Cressida,* do not seem to be true of the tragedies when the plays are judged in their totality and in relation to their effect on an audience.

NOTES TO CHAPTER FIVE

¹Brooke, *John Webster . . .* , p. 128.

²*WD,* IV, ii, 224 ff.

³Lucas, I, 25. Lucas, in II, 140, n. to I, i, 532, notes the atmosphere of mortality that broods over the scene.

NOTE TO CHAPTER SIX

¹Martin Sampson suggests of Vittoria's final couplet, "This dying speech is so inferior to Vittoria's preceding speech, that not improbably this one belongs to Zanche, with whose character it is in accord." *The White Devil and The Duchess of Malfi,* ed. Martin Sampson (Boston, 1906), p. 205. Zanche, however, probably dies silent at line 253; even if she did not, it is much more important that the leading character make the final statement of the main theme than that a lascivious, unprincipled servant be allowed to preach. Indeed, Zanche is one to be avoided with the courts, not one to preach avoidance. Actually, the couplet is not much in accord with anybody's character. It is a final thematic statement, put for emphasis in the mouth of an important character.

NOTE TO CONCLUSION

¹W. B. Yeats, "Emotion of Multitude," *Essays* (New York, The Macmillan Co., 1924), pp. 266–267. This material is used with the permission of The Macmillan Company.